Footprints
in the
Holy Land

◄ A Devotional Discovery Guide ►

Linden D. Kirby

Footprints in the Holy Land
Copyright © 1998 by Linden D. Kirby

Discovery House Publishers is affiliated with RBC Ministries,
Grand Rapids, Michigan 49512

Unless indicated otherwise, Scripture quotations are from the
Holy Bible: New International Version, copyright © 1973, 1978,
1984 International Bible Society. Used by permission of
Zondervan Bible Publishers.

Scripture quotations marked NRSV are from the New Revised
Standard Version.

Scripture quotations marked KJV are from the King James
Version.

Library of Congress Cataloging-in-Publication Data

Kirby, Linden D., 1951–
     Footprints in the Holy Land : a devotional discovery
  guide / by Linden D. Kirby.
     p. cm.
  Includes indexes.

    ISBN 1-57293-028-4

1. Christian shrines—Palestine—Meditations. 2. Christian
antiquities—Palestine—Meditations. 3. Palestine—Antiquities.
4. Palestine—Church history. 5. Palestine—Description and
travel. 6. Excavations (Antiquities)—Palestine. I. Title.
BV896.P19K57   1997
263'.0425694—dc21   97-38199
                                     CIP

Printed in the United States of America

98 00 02 03 01 99
CHG
1 3 5 7 9 10 8 6 4 2

Photo credits see page 227

For LITSA,
my wife, my helper, my best friend

And for LAUREN and LESLEY,
my daughters and greatest supporters

CONTENTS

JERUSALEM

JUDEA & SAMARIA

GALILEE

W hile it is still true today that "of making many books there is no end" (Ecclesiastes 12:12), here is a book that is truly unique. *Footprints in the Holy Land* enables us to visualize the places of the Holy Land without setting foot in the land of Israel. Combining relevant meditations and illuminating photography, it changes mere names and locations into living people and places. Turning its pages, readers will be tempted to exclaim, "It's almost like being there."

For those who will never be able to travel to the places included here, this book will serve as an armchair guide to the Holy Land. But for those who have the privilege of visiting Israel, this book will make the experience even more meaningful and memorable.

There are, of course, many books available to orient and enrich your understanding of this historically and spiritually important land, but *Footprints in the Holy Land* will prove uniquely helpful.

Vernon Grounds

Jerusalem

The Not-So-Handsome Prince

During his lifetime Absalom had taken a pillar and erected it in the King's Valley as a monument to himself, for he thought, "I have no son to carry on the memory of my name." He named the pillar after himself, and it is called Absalom's Monument to this day.

2 Samuel 18:18

Beautiful on the outside but empty on the inside, Absalom's Pillar symbolizes the life of Israel's popular prince.

Take a moment to play a word association game. Think of one key character trait for each of these four men: Noah, Abraham, Moses, David. Do words such as *obedient, faithful, meek,* and *godly* come to mind?

Now describe the character of Absalom. He was ambitious, rebellious, stubborn, sly, and vain. While his physical features were flawless, Absalom's inner man was ugly. His character defects made him a not-so-handsome prince.

Perhaps his attractiveness was even a liability. Could it be that the king's son failed to develop inner beauty because he saw no need for it? His good looks and charm carried him so far that he never recognized the value of integrity, honor, and truth.

Absalom's vanity compelled him to build a monument to himself in his own lifetime. Of course, memorials are usually erected, after one's death, by surviving family and friends. But apparently Absalom's three sons had already died (2 Samuel 14:27). So Absalom, wanting to be certain of enduring fame, erected a pillar to his own name in the King's Valley. He probably intended it as a magnificent marker for his grave.

But Absalom died without dignity. While fleeing his father's supporters, he rode under an oak tree and caught his hair in the low-hanging branches. While suspended between heaven and earth, he was murdered by a former friend. Then, instead of being laid to rest with pomp and circumstance, Absalom's body was dumped in a pit and buried under a pile of rocks (2 Samuel 18:17).

Somewhere east of Jerusalem that day there was a grand and glorious monument meant to enshrine the body of the king's son. No one went there to mourn. No one seemed to care how beautiful it looked. Absalom's Pillar stood unoccupied, a fitting symbol for the man who himself was but an empty shell.

Lord, let me concentrate on developing the inner beauty of character, whose testimony will outlast any monument made of stone.

The King's Valley, where Absalom erected his monument, is today identified with the Kidron Valley, which runs along the east side of Jerusalem, separating the Temple Mount and the Mount of Olives. There in this valley, just below the southeast corner of the city wall, stands a curious structure with a conical roof, popularly know as Absalom's Pillar. Rising 47 feet (14 m) high, its base is a solid piece of rock cut and carved from the limestone slope. In the heart of the limestone block is a hand-hewn room approximately 8 feet x 8 feet (2.5 m x 2.5 m) with two burial shelves.

Despite its name, hardly anyone believes this to be the actual pillar that Absalom erected to his own memory. The architecture, as well as that of the nearby St. James' Grotto and Zechariah's Tomb, is clearly that of centuries later. The original Absalom's Pillar was apparently destroyed long ago.

ENRICHMENT

"Years I spent in vanity and pride," wrote the hymnwriter William R. Newell. It is healthy for us to admit the same. Absalom's sins were many, but we must confess that we, too, are subject to the same desires. "A person's pride will bring humiliation, but one who is lowly in spirit will obtain honor" (Proverbs 29:23 NRSV).

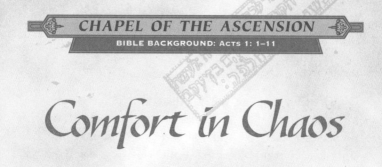

Comfort in Chaos

"Men of Galilee," they said, "why do you stand here look-ing into the sky? This same Jesus, who has been taken from you into heaven, will come back in the same way you have seen him go into heaven."

Acts 1:11

The tiny Chapel of the Ascension sits atop the Mount of Olives.

There is nothing more aggravating than a "new and improved" product that is inferior to the old one. Once we have become accustomed to something, we don't like people messing with it. We enjoy predictability.

There is comfort in the familiar and solace in sameness. This is especially true when our personal world is in chaos. We feel more secure when important people and places remain the same.

When Jesus ascended into the sky and left His disciples speechlessly staring into heaven, two angels offered a message of comfort. This *same* Jesus would come back in the *same* way they had seen Him go.

This *same* Jesus would return. Not a different Jesus. Not a "new and improved" Jesus—but the same one they had come to know and love while He was with them.

Thus, Jesus' authoritative words, "I tell you the truth," would again guide them. His "Take courage! It is I. Don't be afraid" would again encourage them. His eyes of love would again accept them.

And this same Jesus would return in the *same* way as He had gone. His bodily ascension foretold His bodily return. The voice that had bid the weary, "Come to me," would summon sinners once again. The nail-scarred hands would again reach out to the doubting.

While the ascension of Christ upset the disciples' world, there was hope that the future would be manageable because this same Jesus would someday return. The promise of predictability brought comfort in chaos.

In the midst of my confusion, I pray to the one who is the same yesterday, today, and forever. May I know the comfort of your unchanging character and the peace of your personal presence.

INSIGHT

On the western side of the Mount of Olives stands a tiny domed building inside the confines of a mosque. The Chapel of the Ascension is supposedly built on the spot where Christ ascended into heaven. Inside, the trusting tourist may see a mark on the floor said to be Jesus' footprint. Of course, few believe the tale. The tradition of this place is no older than the Crusader period.

The actual location of Christ's ascension is unknown. The best that biblical scholars can do is to combine the geographical information Luke gives in his two accounts. Acts 1:12 points to the Mount of Olives, and Luke 24:50–51 indicates the vicinity of Bethany. Therefore, the ascension must have taken place somewhere on the eastern side of the Mount of Olives close to Bethany.

ENRICHMENT

The way to commemorate the ascension is to look *up*, not down. The Bible tells us Jesus was taken up in a cloud, and it indicates that He will come again in the clouds (see Matthew 24:30, 26:64; Mark 13:26, 14:62). Keeping an eye on the clouds is more biblical than searching for His final footprint.

However, the disciples were rebuked for gazing skyward too long. In anticipation of His return, we are challenged by the last words of Christ Himself: "But you will receive power when the Holy Spirit comes on you; and you will be my witnesses in Jerusalem, and in all Judea and in Samaria, and to the ends of the earth" (Acts 1:8).

Witnessing for Christ in your own "Jerusalem" is a beautiful way to remember Jesus' parting command and anticipate His glorious return.

Depth of Denial

The Lord turned and looked straight at Peter. Then Peter remembered the word the Lord had spoken to him: "Before the rooster crows today, you will disown me three times."

Luke 22:61

A bronze statue of a rooster looks down on recent renovations at the Church of St. Peter in Gallicantu.

Peter was famous for his brash statements and bold actions. And there in the courtyard of the high priest, his brashness came home to roost. It caught up with him and humbled him. He found out how truly weak he was.

Just hours earlier, in the safe and secure environment of the Upper Room, surrounded by friends, Peter had declared, "Lord, I am ready to go with you to prison and to death" (Luke 22:33). Then later, in the cold night, surrounded by strangers and possible enemies, Peter could not summon the same confidence.

His seemingly iron resolve to be faithful to Jesus had melted away under the low heat of simple questioning. He did not stand up for Jesus. He was intimidated by a servant girl. He was afraid of an unknown fellow. And he was threatened when he was correctly identified.

Peter's problem went deeper than his public denial of Christ. Serious as it was—and triply serious for its repetition—his denial of his Master was the result of another hidden denial. Peter had gotten himself into this predicament because he had denied the power of his own sin nature.

The prophet Jeremiah warned, "The heart is deceitful above all things and beyond cure. Who can understand it?" (Jeremiah 17:9). Peter's real problem was that he failed to reckon on the desperate wickedness of his own heart. The depth of that personal, spiritual denial was the cause of his public denial of Christ.

Had this outspoken disciple been willing to admit his spiritual weakness, surely Jesus would have granted him strength to remain loyal. But it was precisely because Peter thought he could do it on his own that Jesus allowed him to fail. When he trusted his heart's passion instead of God's enabling, he set himself up for failure.

We get into trouble the same way. Many times we *want* to be faithful. The heart says, "I will," and we make declarations based on our own determination. Too late we discover that while our intention is perfect, our execution is poor.

We must learn from Peter's denial and face the depths of our own inabilities. When we admit the worst in ourselves, we will rely utterly upon God. It is then we will be enabled to do our best.

All-knowing and infinitely understanding Father, I freely admit I am like Peter. If I learn anything from his denial, it is that I must face the worst in myself. I turn to you. Enable me to carry out my good spiritual intentions because I am trusting in your strength.

INSIGHT

The Church of St. Peter in Gallicantu was built in 1931 on top of first-century ruins thought by some to be the remains of one of Caiaphas' houses. *Gallicantu* is a Latin word meaning "cockcrow" or "at the place where the cock crows." Today, you may still hear a rooster crowing. Let it be a reminder not only of Peter's denial but also of our own spiritual frailty.

ENRICHMENT

Jesus was condemned, abused, and kept overnight at the house of Caiaphas. If this is the correct identification of the site, then the ancient Maccabean steps in the courtyard are certainly those that Jesus Himself trod during His final night.

Although visitors are restricted from these steps, you can, in your mind's eye, see Jesus walking there. With each silent step, He climbed closer to His fateful confrontation with the Jewish religious leaders. With each step He inched nearer to His final condemnation on our behalf.

Beneath the present-day church is a dungeon. Careful examination reveals holes bored through the stone columns. These probably indicate where prisoners such as Jesus were tied. He was blindfolded, mocked, and beaten. It is a sobering experience to stand where Jesus may have stood, knowing He bore it all for us.

An Empty Tomb

"He is not here; he has risen, just as he said. Come and see the place where he lay."

Matthew 28:6

The simplicity of the Garden Tomb and its peaceful gardens help the seeker focus on Jesus and the awesome power of His resurrection.

The greatest news ever heard was announced in a garden outside an empty tomb. The angel told Mary Magdalene that Jesus was alive! "He has risen, just as he said." Then he invited Mary to investigate the evidence for the resurrection.

With your own eyes you can see some of these same evidences as they apply to the Garden Tomb. While it cannot be proved that this is the place where Jesus was laid, it is enlightening to discover more than a dozen scriptural requirements that the Garden Tomb fulfills. Seven of these are found in John's record.

First, John noted that the place of Jesus' burial was very near the place of His crucifixion (19:41–42). The Garden Tomb was close enough to Gordon's Calvary that two men could have carried Jesus' body to this place.

John made much of the fact that the tomb of Jesus was in a garden (19:41; 20:15). No garden could have grown in this arid climate without irrigation in the summer. At the site of the Garden Tomb several cisterns have been discovered. One of them can hold 200,000 gallons (900,000 l) of water, making it the third largest cistern in Jerusalem! These cisterns would have provided more than enough water to support a thriving vineyard and many trees.

Third, John noted that Jesus' body was placed in a new tomb, in which no one else had been laid. Although the Garden Tomb had spaces for two bodies, apparently only one location was ever finished. The foot niche chiseled from the end of the burial place on the far wall indicates that one as the occupied space.

Fourth, when Mary Magdalene came to the tomb on the first Easter morning, she found the stone gone from the entrance. Jesus' tomb had been closed by rolling a huge stone over the opening. The groove in front of the Garden Tomb's doorway indicates it also may have been sealed by such a rolling stone.

Fifth, the writer provided an additional eyewitness detail. John said that the disciple who arrived at the tomb ahead of Peter had to bend over to look inside the tomb. Commonly the entrances to tombs of the first century were small, making them easier to close off and secure. The original doorway into the Garden Tomb was only about 4 feet (1.2 m) high.

From his vantage point outside the tomb entrance, the disciple was able to see Jesus' resting place and the forsaken burial cloths. The design of the Garden Tomb also permits such an unobstructed view. From the doorway, one can easily see over the low wall and straight through to the far burial space.

Finally, the Garden Tomb was empty! Thus it met the most vital requirement for the tomb of Jesus. Jesus arose from the dead! An empty tomb is plain and simple evidence of the truth the angels proclaimed: "He is not here; he has risen, just as he said."

Here in this garden I praise you, Jesus, as my resurrected Savior and living Lord! You left behind an empty tomb proving your power over death. I find hope and joy in the new life you bring.

INSIGHT

Jesus was crucified and buried outside the city walls. The writer to the Hebrews affirms that Jesus "suffered outside the city gate to make the people holy through his own blood" (13:12). The site of Gordon's Calvary and the Garden Tomb is located outside Jerusalem's present north wall. Thus, it apparently meets a key requirement for the location of the crucifixion and resurrection of Christ.

However, a second possible site must also be considered. The Church of the Holy Sepulchre, while definitely inside the present city wall, may have been outside the north wall during the first century. So the Church of the Holy Sepulchre also meets this test of authenticity.

The question of the location of Christ's tomb must be decided by more than one factor alone. Unfortunately, the issue may never be settled.

ENRICHMENT

For many Christian pilgrims, the Garden Tomb is the highlight of their Holy Land visit. Prepare your heart before you arrive. Let nothing get in the way of meeting the resurrected Christ here in this peaceful garden.

It is a thrilling experience to celebrate the resurrection of Jesus Christ with communion at the Garden Tomb. This serene setting provides an unforgettable backdrop to a very meaningful encounter with Christ. Advance arrangements assure that your hosts will have everything ready when you arrive.

If you have opportunity to visit Bethlehem before you go to the Garden Tomb, you can get olive wood communion cups there. They can provide a tangible remembrance of this once-in-a-lifetime spiritual experience.

Choose Your Gate

Enter through the narrow gate. . . that leads to life.

Matthew 7:13–14

Stone lions on the walls near the top of the archway guard the Lions' Gate, which opens to the Via Dolorosa northeast of the Temple Mount.

Contestants on a popular television game show are offered a choice of three doors. They know that if they choose correctly, they will receive a fabulous prize. But if they choose incorrectly, they may end up with something they do not want.

In Old Jerusalem today, the visitor is presented with eight gates from which to choose. Each gate leads the traveler to a different place. The gate one chooses determines one's destination.

Jesus presented His listeners with a similar choice—the wide gate or the narrow gate. But there were no secrets or surprises here. He told them plainly what lay behind each gate.

The most popular choice is the wide gate that opens onto a broad and easy road. It looks like an expressway to fun and happiness. It is a parkway of pleasure that appeals to the sinful nature. It looks delightful, but it ends in destruction. With thousands thronging this thoroughfare, it seems to be the right way, but people pursuing this route ignore God and slip into hell without a Savior.

The other choice does not appear to be as good as the more popular choice. This gate is tight and leads to a narrow path. It requires the entrant to unload his possessions and go through with no claim to anything of value. There aren't as many people traveling this path. And those who do go this way do not travel without struggle, suffering, or self-denial. The way is sprinkled with the blood of Christ and the martyrs.

Yet this is the way that Jesus tells us to choose. This is the way that leads to the pearly gates of heaven and takes us to the very throne of God. The psalmist says "You have made known to me the path of life; you will fill me with joy in your presence, with eternal pleasures at your right hand" (Psalm 16:11).

Choose your gate carefully. Decide whether the wide or the narrow one is what you want. But realize that your earthly choice will determine your eternal destination.

Lord Jesus, I choose the narrow gate that leads to life. I know it is the way of the cross that leads me to heaven.

The eight gates of Old Jerusalem fascinate students of the Bible and history alike. Here they are listed clockwise from the southeast.

The *Dung Gate* leads to the Western Wall and the Temple area. The present gate is not the same as the ancient Dung Gate mentioned in Nehemiah 3:14. This one was built no earlier than A.D. 70.

The *Zion Gate* is sometimes called the "Jewish Quarter Gate" because it is much used by the residents of that section of the city. Its face is deeply pitted with bullet holes from the 1948 and 1967 wars.

The *Jaffa Gate,* on the west, is the most used entrance into the Old City. Fortified by David's Tower, it is one of the most imposing and significant gates. Originally it was the starting point for the road to Jaffa, a busy port and trade center.

The *New Gate,* at the northwestern corner, was first opened in 1887. (Anything in Jerusalem that is less than two hundred years old is still "new.")

The *Damascus Gate,* on the north, marks the connection between the Old City and the ancient road to Damascus, Syria. Considered by many the most beautiful gate because of its ornate turrets, it is still an observation point used by Israeli security forces.

Herod's Gate is so named because someone misidentified a nearby church as the home of Herod Antipas. It leads into the Muslim Quarter.

The *Lions' Gate,* on the east, takes its name from the pairs of lions carved on either side of the arched entrance. It is also sometimes identified as St. Stephen's Gate because tradition indicates that he was martyred nearby (Acts 7:57-58).

The *Golden Gate* holds much significance for Jews and Christians alike. Many Jews believe their Messiah will someday enter the Temple Mount through this eastern gate facing the Mount of Olives. Christians believe He already has! Logically this would be the gate through which Jesus entered the city on Palm Sunday. It was blocked up by the Muslims in 1530 and remains sealed today. However, Christians await the day of Christ's return when many believe He will enter the Holy City again through this beautiful gate (see *Golden Gate*, p. 33).

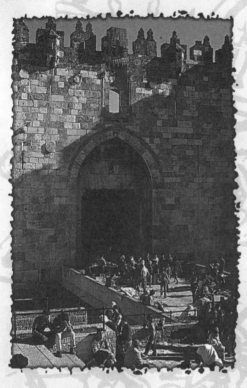

The Damascus Gate leads into the Old City from East Jerusalem and has provided a landmark for locals and pilgrims for nearly five centuries.

ENRICHMENT

The Sermon on the Mount (Matthew 5–7) was delivered on a hillside in Galilee, not in Jerusalem. Therefore, it is unlikely that Jesus had any specific gates in mind when He spoke of the narrow and wide gates. Besides, those seen today, with the exception of the New Gate, were all built by Suleiman the Magnificent in the early sixteenth century. Nonetheless, these grand stone structures serve well as symbols of the spiritual gates Jesus taught about.

When you pass through these arches, pause for a moment and observe the people who scurry around you. Pray that many here may find Jesus who is the Way, the Truth, and the Life.

Agony All Alone

And being in anguish, he prayed more earnestly, and his sweat was like drops of blood falling to the ground.

Luke 22:44

The gnarled olive trees in Gethsemane's garden provide a living link to the ancient groves that covered the Mount of Olives in Jesus' day.

There is dynamite wrapped in this page of Luke's gospel—emotional dynamite. These short verses are packed with powerful concepts. They give us glimpses of the anguish Jesus experienced in Gethsemane the night of His betrayal.

Knowing that the cross stood in the road ahead of Him, Jesus stepped aside for a few hours to pray. His prayer was simple: "Father, if you are willing, take this cup from me; yet not my will, but yours be done." He asked that if there were another way to bring redemption to mankind it would be revealed. He would have avoided the horrors of crucifixion and the agony of separation from the Father if at all possible.

Luke emphasized the depth of Jesus' torment with three revealing details. First, of the four gospel writers, only Luke recorded that an angel came to strengthen Jesus. Think of it—the Creator of angels receives assistance from one of His creations. Such heaven-sent angelic aid indicates that the Father understood His Son's anguish even when no one else could.

Second, Dr. Luke stated matter-of-factly that Jesus' sweat was like drops of blood falling to the ground. This condition, hematidrosis, results from the rupture of capillaries near the surface of the skin. Severe anguish and mental stress cause this rare condition in which blood is released through the sweat glands. Jesus' spiritual anguish was so deep it literally tore Him up physically.

Third, while Jesus' friends were physically present, they were emotionally absent. They failed Him when He needed them most.

Jesus' heart was broken in Gethsemane. He saw what He had to do, and He understood that He had to do it alone. The suffering He endured in the garden prepared Him for the cross.

Suffering Savior, though I cannot comprehend the depth of your agony, I can appreciate the strength of your resolve. I am forever grateful that you drained the bitter cup for me.

INSIGHT

Gethsemane comes from an Aramaic word meaning "oil-press." All we know for certain about the garden's location is that it is on the Mount of Olives, just east of the Kidron Valley.

There are four places that vie for the honor of being known as the place of Jesus' spiritual agony. Most popular is the garden grove of ancient olive trees adjacent to the Basilica of the Agony. This Roman Catholic church, also called the Church of All Nations, houses the traditional Rock of the Agony where Jesus knelt (Luke 22:41).

Just north of the church is the Tomb of the Virgin. Although the church itself was built in the fifth century, to the right of its entrance is a cave that has an older tradition. The cave is now housed in a building, and it has been altered considerably from its original condition; however, excavations conducted in the 1950s uncovered evidence that it once housed an olive press—perhaps two. A strong case can be made for the authenticity of this spot as the location of Jesus' agony.

A third and a fourth option are also nearby. The Greek Orthodox Church claims a site to the east. And farther up the hill, adjacent to the Church of Mary Magdalene, the Russian Orthodox maintain a large and peaceful grove they call Gethsemane.

While further study about each of these sites would be enlightening, it would likely be inconclusive. The best approach is to enter Gethsemane with a heart of faith. With this attitude you may be certain to find Jesus, regardless of the location you choose.

ENRICHMENT

Because there is so much to see in the Holy Land, many who start out as pilgrims end up as mere tourists. They take home pictures but no spiritual experiences. Gethsemane is a place where you can still find Jesus. He waits for those who seek Him, but He hides from those who hurry.

Pray that you will not fall into temptation. Find a quiet place. Take a few minutes. Encounter Christ.

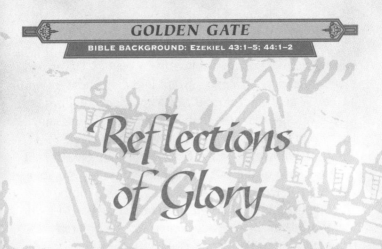

GOLDEN GATE

BIBLE BACKGROUND: Ezekiel 43:1–5; 44:1–2

Reflections of Glory

The glory of the Lord entered the temple through the gate facing east.

Ezekiel 43:4

The sealed double arches of the Golden Gate will one day open to welcome Christ as He returns to set up His kingdom on earth.

Today the Golden Gate's weathered face glows in the glory of the rising sun. Through the ages its twin arches have welcomed kings and common folk alike to the holy temple mount. And now, though blocked and sealed, the legends of glory still cling to its tawny face.

Almost certainly Jesus passed through this grand gate at the climax of His triumphal entry into Jerusalem on

Palm Sunday. Jesus rode down the Mount of Olives and then "entered Jerusalem and went into the temple" (Mark 11:11). Since this is the only gate leading directly from the Mount of Olives into the temple, it is universally assumed Jesus used this eastern gate during His final week.

Today, however, attention focuses on the Golden Gate because of the role it will play in the second coming of Christ. Ezekiel saw a vision of the glory of the Lord entering the temple through "the gate facing east" (43:4). Many students of prophecy interpret this reference as being fulfilled in the second coming of Christ.

When Jesus returns, His feet will touch the Mount of Olives and He will proceed into Jerusalem. His second triumphal entry will again take Him through this magnificent gate. The "appearing of our great God and Savior, Jesus Christ" is the blessed hope of every believer (Titus 2:13).

Will your heart be open and ready for the Lord's return? Or will He find it blocked by materialism and sealed by sin? The apostle John admonishes us saying, "And now, dear children, continue in him, so that when he appears we may be confident and unashamed before him at his coming" (1 John 2:28).

To be confident and unashamed, we must remove every known sin and purify each dark corner. Then we can rejoice in Jesus' return knowing we ourselves are prepared to reflect His glory.

Lord of Glory, I await your return. I am ready to welcome you. May my life reflect your glory.

INSIGHT

The eastern gate seen today was built during the Byzantine Period, but directly below it is an older gate now completely hidden from view. Although scholars argue about the age of this gate, some make a convincing case for the likelihood that it was built by King Solomon. If so, this Lower Gate is most certainly the very one through which Jesus entered the Temple on Palm Sunday.

Viewed from the Temple Mount, the western side of the Golden Gate shows more of its impressive majesty.

Today's Byzantine double-arched gate is mortared shut. Most believe this was done during the sixteenth century by the Ottoman Turks sometime after Suleiman the Magnificent buttressed and restored it on the western side. Why was it sealed? Legend supplies the motivation. Knowing the Jewish and Christian belief that the Messiah would enter Jerusalem through this gate, the Moslem governor had it walled up in order to block His coming. But praise God, no masonry is strong enough to prohibit Jesus the Messiah's return.

ENRICHMENT

Every year millions of visitors view the Golden Gate's east face from the Mount of Olives. This is the only side that exists in the minds of most. However, more of this magnificent structure is visible from the Temple Mount.

From the west you will gain a better perspective of the gate's size and beauty. Note the perpendicular arches added by Suleiman to shore up the gate's leaning facade. Notice also the central pillar between the arches. According to tradition, the columns that separate the two gate chambers were a gift to King Solomon from the Queen of Sheba.

Room For More

For God so loved the world that he gave his one and only Son,
that whoever believes in him shall not perish but have eternal life.

John 3:16

With a little imagination, one can see the sunken eye sockets and eroded nose of a human skull on the limestone face of Gordon's Calvary.

There was a crowd at the foot of the cross. Seven groups and individuals clustered close by. Each had a purpose and a story to tell.

Simon the Cyrene carried Jesus' cross. Certainly he had not planned on spending his morning that way. Probably he fulfilled his obligation grudgingly. Nonetheless, Jesus needed someone, and Simon did the job.

The Roman soldiers were following orders—just doing their job. In discharging their duties, they crucified an innocent man, but who was to care? It was all in a day's work. They were the pawns of the powerful.

The Jewish religious leaders were the real power brokers orchestrating Jesus' crucifixion. For them, Jesus' death was a personal and political victory. He was a troublemaker who got in the way. Now He was eliminated.

A robber hung on either side of Jesus. These men were guilty of their crimes and deserved to die. One saw his spiritual need and turned to Christ as Savior. The other refused to admit his need and used Jesus in a last attempt to elevate himself by putting another down.

The passersby blasphemed and went on their merry way. They had no concept of what really was happening. They viewed the crucifixion as one last chance to kick a man when he was down. They understood Jesus' prophetic words and ministry superficially. They fancied themselves well-informed, but they missed the point altogether.

According to Matthew and Mark, many women, not just a few, were also at Golgotha. Love for Jesus brought them there. They had followed Jesus on a path of dedicated service. Now the end of the road brought them to the cross.

Finally, although Matthew doesn't mention him, John also witnessed the crucifixion. He is the only apostle to risk exposure, capture, and personal martyrdom to stand faithfully by the side of his Lord. Because of John's devotion, Jesus entrusted him with the care of His own mother, Mary.

Seven groups and individuals huddled at the foot of the cross. Do you see yourself there, too? With which group do you stand?

No matter how crowded it is at the cross, there is always room for one more.

Lord Jesus Christ, I stand at the foot of your cross. I see your sacrifice and accept your death for me. Show me the place of service you have for me.

INSIGHT

Matthew, Mark, and John use the Aramaic word *Golgotha*, "the place of the skull," to identify the place where Jesus died. Luke calls it simply by its Greek name, *the Skull* (or *Calvary* in KJV).

No one knows how the place got its name. Some speculate that it was because the place resembled a skull. Others say it was an execution site; thus, human skulls were commonplace.

Neither archeology nor history can prove where Golgotha is located. Two sites, however, are favored.

The first carries the weight of tradition dating to the fourth century. While excavating the site of Jesus' tomb, a piece of Christ's cross supposedly was found. Claims of miraculous healings effected by this relic seemed to authenticate the site of the crucifixion. Today the Roman Catholic Church teaches that both the tomb of Jesus and the place of His crucifixion may be visited inside the Church of the Holy Sepulchre.

Many Protestants point to a skull-shaped rocky knoll northeast of the Damascus Gate as the most likely site for Golgotha. It is named Gordon's Calvary after General Charles Gordon, who found the tomb in 1882 and suggested that it was the site of Christ's crucifixion.

Pros and cons of each location can be argued. Dense building in the area prevents further excavation; thus, the issue may never be settled. As with other holy events, however, knowing *where* it happened is not as important as knowing *that* it happened.

ENRICHMENT

Since you are likely to visit both Gordon's Calvary and the Church of the Holy Sepulchre, you can make your own observations of each site. Where do you sense the presence of Jesus? Why do you favor the one location over the other?

When you return home, perhaps you will want to study the issue further.

Hell on Earth

"Then he will say to those on his left, 'Depart from me, you who are cursed, into the eternal fire prepared for the devil and his angels.'"

Matthew 25:41

Today the Hinnom Valley looks like a nice place for a family outing.

The Hinnom Valley is a steep-sided ravine that wraps around the southern end of Mount Zion on the south side of Old Jerusalem. It is a pretty park where parents bring their children for summer concerts, food, and fun. All the horrors of by-gone years are hidden beneath the sod and the cloak of history.

Here in Old Testament times children were burned alive as sacrifices to Baal. In New Testament times this valley was the place for burning rubbish, dead animals, and even the bodies of criminals. It was a place of decay, putrefaction, continual fire, and death.

Jesus used the Greek word *Gehenna* (a transliteration of the Hebrew words meaning "Valley of Hinnom") as a symbol of the eternal punishment prepared for the devil, his angels, and the wicked. Our modern Bible versions simply call it *hell*.

The Hinnom Valley today gives no evidence of its despicable past. Apparently no one wants to think about it. It is as if by refusing to acknowledge the hellish horrors of yesterday, one can deny the reality of hell for today and tomorrow.

But Christians operate with a different perspective. Jesus taught that hell is a place of unquenchable fire, continual weeping, and gnashing of teeth. It is a place certainly to be avoided!

Our responsibility is to warn the hell-bound. Their ignorance and complacency must be interrupted by loving confrontations with the truth. Only by exposing the realities of hell can we hope to "snatch others from the fire and save them" (Jude 23).

O God, help me not only to acknowledge the reality of hell but to be motivated by it to a clear and compelling witness. Help me to turn others to Jesus the Savior.

INSIGHT

At the southeastern end of the Hinnom Valley the Haceldama Monastery sits on the traditional site of the Field of Blood. (*Haceldama* is the Greek translation of the Hebrew for "field of blood.") This is the plot of ground bought with the blood money Judas received for betraying Jesus (Acts 1:18–19). Its location in the Hinnom Valley just adds to the evil associations of this godforsaken place.

ENRICHMENT

Most tours do not stop in the Hinnom Valley, but they cross it on the way to or from other sites. Your guide may point it out. However, if you have the opportunity to stroll along its banks, be sure to note the atmosphere. Do you sense an ambiance of fun and frivolity? Or an air of foreboding?

Under His Wings

> "O Jerusalem, Jerusalem, you who kill the prophets and stone those sent to you, how often I have longed to gather your children together, as a hen gathers her chicks under her wings, but you were not willing!"
>
> Luke 13:34

Jerusalem, the capital of Israel, still draws the world to her gates.

In its three-thousand-year history as the capital of Israel, Jerusalem has been attacked, besieged, conquered, and divided more than forty times. Today it is caught in a tug-of-war between Arabs and Israelis, Muslims and Jews, Protestants and Catholics. Yet ironically, it is called "The City of Peace."

Since the day in 1004 B.C. when David captured and named it his capital, Jerusalem has been the focus of international conflict. Its position at the crossroads of world empires has made it the natural battlefield for nations wishing to control the area. Old Jerusalem is divided into four quarters: Jewish, Armenian, Muslim, and Christian. And three great world religions—Judaism, Christianity, and Islam—all lay claim to its holy sites.

Such diversity inevitably brings discord, and discord brings pain to the heart of God. Jesus revealed His compassion for the people of Jerusalem when He likened His concern to that of a mother hen. Just as chicks find security under the wings of the mother hen, so God's children experience love, peace, and salvation in Christ.

But the people of Jerusalem spurned the offer of Christ. They refused to take spiritual shelter. Instead, they went on with their own agendas, pecking and scratching for peace that would not satisfy.

In His life, Jesus displayed compassion for the physical and mental needs of people. He healed the sick and freed the oppressed. In His death, He granted eternal salvation to all who come to Him. No one is refused. Regardless of race, nationality, or religious background, whosoever will, may come.

Jerusalem remains a city of political turmoil and spiritual restlessness. Without Christ, unity is improbable, and peace is impossible. Yet the divine desire endures. Jesus the Messiah still longs to gather all Jerusalem under His saving wings.

Lord, I rejoice to know salvation and protection under your wings. May many in this city of complexity and confusion also come to you.

INSIGHT

According to the Talmud, "When the world was created, it received ten measures of beauty, and nine fell on Jerusalem."

Without a doubt, Jerusalem is a jewel. It especially sparkles under the slanting rays of the morning sun. It is then that it most deserves the title, "Jerusalem the Golden."

By requiring every new building be faced with local white limestone, the city fathers have attempted to unify ancient and modern architecture. This white face reflects the sun and makes the city glow.

ENRICHMENT

What can one person do in a city of nearly six hundred thousand that knows no peace? Become an agent of peace.

If you ask God to show you how to make a spiritual difference in this holy city, He will. Some people go "prayer walking." Some take Hebrew New Testaments and leave them in hotel rooms. Others find opportunities for witness with people they meet. The Holy Spirit is seeking sensitive saints to be His agents of peace wherever they go.

Ben Yehuda Street in modern Jerusalem bustles with life.

Moving Day

On that day his feet will stand on the Mount of Olives, east of Jerusalem, and the Mount of Olives will be split in two from east to west, forming a great valley, with half of the mountain moving north and half moving south.

Zechariah 14:4

Churches built to memorialize sacred events in the life of Christ now dot the western slope of the Mount of Olives. On the left, the Church of All Nations marks the traditional place of Jesus' agony in Gethsemane.

Jesus spent many days and many nights on the Mount of Olives. Here He taught His disciples, raised Lazarus, began His triumphal procession on Palm Sunday, and wept over Jerusalem. Significant events of the final week took place on its slopes. Here also He agonized in Gethsemane, and from this mount, He ascended to the Father.

Although Christ has now gone into heaven, He is not finished with the Mount of Olives. The prophet

Zechariah tells of an event yet to be realized that will take place on this mountain—Jesus' coming again!

On the Day of the Lord, Jesus will descend to earth again, this time as the victorious Judge and Ruler. His feet will touch the Mount of Olives, and it actually will split in two.

Scientists report that a great earthquake fault runs through this range of hills east of Jerusalem. Perhaps the second coming of Christ will trigger a great natural catastrophe that will change the face of the Holy City and its surrounding geography. By whatever means, the present mount will open up, and a new valley will be formed.

On that day of the Lord's return, all the world will be forever altered. The most far-reaching changes will be spiritual. With His dramatic touchdown on the Mount of Olives, the Messiah will begin His reign in human hearts. "The Lord will be king over the whole earth," Zechariah says. "On that day there will be one Lord, and his name the only name" (14:9).

When our Lord Jesus Christ returns to stand on the Mount of Olives, He will literally shake the earth. And He will move its inhabitants in a way they have never been moved before.

Lord, speed the day of your return. This old world needs to be shaken.

INSIGHT

The Mount of Olives, without a doubt, received its name in a day when olive trees flourished on its slopes. Today, there may be more religious shrines, churches, and chapels on the hillside than olive trees. To name them all would take several paragraphs; to annotate them, pages; to properly appreciate them, days. Content yourself with highlights of those that you and your guide determine to be the most critical for your spiritual pilgrimage.

ENRICHMENT

From the Mount of Olives, just below the Seven Arches Hotel, you can experience a breathtaking panorama of Jerusalem. It is a view not to be missed. You will want to take pictures, of course, and this is one place where a wide-angle lens comes closest to capturing the real splendor of the scene. If you don't have a wide-angle lens, don't worry. An enterprising local will sell you a 1 x 3-foot (.3 x 1 m) print for a dollar.

This overlook is so popular with visitors, it inevitably draws those who make their livelihood from tourists. So, have your dollars ready. You may buy postcards or take a camel ride. Just don't be taken in if someone offers you a ride on a donkey he claims is a direct descendant of the one Jesus rode on Palm Sunday!

Talking to Our Father

"When you pray, go into your room, close the door and pray to your Father, who is unseen. Then your Father, who sees what is done in secret, will reward you."

Matthew 6:6

Dur Father who art in heaven, hallowed be thy name, thy kingdom come. Thy will be done in earth as it is in heaven. Give us this day our daily bread. And forgive us our trespasses, as we forgive them that trespass against us. And lead us not into temptation, but deliver us from evil. Amen.

The world's most famous prayer is spoken, sung, and whispered thousands of times daily from the compound of the Pater Noster Church.

Some people think that God likes prayers that are long, loud, and fancy. But the model prayer Jesus taught His disciples was spare and direct. In the context of teaching "The Lord's Prayer," Jesus assured us that the Father hears our prayers because of who He is, not because of our formal presentation.

Prayer is based on a loving relationship. It is the expression of a confident father-and-child connection. Jesus reminds us six times in these few verses that we are praying to our Father. So what is our heavenly Father like?

First, our Father sees the invisible. Therefore we may pray secretly. We may literally close ourselves off from the rest of the world by some means of private retreat, or we may pray mentally without spoken words. Both methods are "secret" prayer. Either way, God understands what is on our hearts. No one else in the universe knows about our prayer, but God does. Because He sees what is done secretly, He is able to answer our private plea.

Second, our Father understands the unspoken. We do not need to offer lengthy explanations of our needs, motives, intentions, and circumstances. In fact, God promises His children, "Before they call I will answer; while they are still speaking I will hear" (Isaiah 65:24). Because the Father knows our needs perfectly, even the shortest prayer can be answered fully.

Because God sees the unseen and hears the unspoken, we pray with confidence. Our heavenly Father hears our prayers no matter how secret or short.

Heavenly Father, even now I breathe a silent prayer, which no one else understands. You know my deepest longings. I bring them confidently to your throne.

INSIGHT

Pater Noster is Latin for "Our Father," the first two words of the Lord's Prayer. Tradition says Jesus taught His disciples that model prayer using the cave on the grounds of the Pater Noster Church as His classroom. Today's visitor finds the Lord's Prayer memorialized in more than eighty languages and inscribed on nearly every wall of the compound. There is even a Braille copy near the entrance.

ENRICHMENT

You will find the English version of the Lord's Prayer in a cloistered passageway of the church. Singing "The Lord's Prayer" there in that hallowed spot is a stirring spiritual experience.

Crippled Thinking

Then Jesus said to him, "Get up! Pick up your mat and walk."
At once the man was cured; he picked up his mat and walked.

John 5:8–9

Gazing down on the ruins of two pools and five colonnades, the visitor can get a sense of the impressive architecture that once made up the Pool of Bethesda.

A paradigm is a way of thinking. It is a mind-set, a pattern we use to make sense of life. We all have many paradigms. We use them every day—especially to navigate uncertain circumstances.

The lame man lying by the Pool of Bethesda had a very powerful paradigm about his potential healing. An invalid for thirty-eight years, his mind-set was ingrained. He thought the only way to health and wholeness was to wash in the agitated waters of this particular pool.

Consider his possible reasons. Most likely he had seen other people healed in these bubbling waters while he struggled to get in. Surely he was inspired by the testimonies of those who had experienced amazing cures. Every time someone else was restored, his hopes rose. *His* limbs could be mended, too, if only he could make it into the water before anyone else. Again and again he told himself, "I can be healed only if I beat the others into the pool."

Along came Jesus with an easy question. "Do you want to get well?" The answer seemed to be obvious, but the lame man did not answer with a simple "yes" or "no." Instead he revealed his personal paradigm of healing by saying, "Sir, I have no one to help me into the pool when the water is stirred. While I am trying to get in, someone else goes down ahead of me."

He thought of healing as coming only by the conventional method. He could not conceive of a cure coming in any other way. His conviction was so strong that he almost missed what he really needed.

Like the lame man, our thinking is crippled by convention, too. We believe the answers to our problems come only in tried-and-true ways. Even our prayers get stuck in the rut of routine reasoning.

Jesus' simple question was an opportunity for the paralytic to check his paradigm. We must do the same. When we view our problems from Jesus' perspective, we may be surprised to find new solutions.

O Lord, I know you often have ways of working that don't fit my expectations. May I be open to new paradigms, so I won't miss the miracles you want to do in my life.

John's gospel is the only one that recorded Jesus' healing of the paralytic by the pool. His description of the place is specific: It was near the Sheep Gate; it was called Bethesda; it was surrounded by five colonnades. In 1888 just such a place was unearthed north of the Temple area in Jerusalem.

The Pool of Bethesda was actually two rectangular pools separated by a stone partition 20 feet (6 m) thick. On this rock wall, the fifth colonnade once stood. The location of these twin pools is deeply engraved with history as well as tradition.

Near these ruins, the Crusaders built the Church of St. Anne. Erected in 1142, it supposedly marks the place where the Virgin Mary's parents lived. When Saladin seized Jerusalem in 1187, the church was used by the Muslims. Despite its return and restoration by Christians, a five-line Arabic inscription still remains over the main door.

ENRICHMENT

The Catholic cloister that surrounds the Church of St. Anne and the Pool of Bethesda offers many refreshing delights to the weary traveler. The cool shade of the pepper trees provides shelter from the scorching sun. Birds send their love songs airmail across the flowered courtyard. The joyful strains of happy pilgrims testing St. Anne's acoustics waft outward and upward over the stone pavement and the ancient pools.

A few moments of tranquillity in this place can do a lot to lift the spirit. A slow song with rich harmony offered to the Lord within the church will echo in your memory forever.

Sent for Cleansing

"Go," he told him, "wash in the pool of Siloam" (this word means Sent). So the man went and washed, and came home seeing.

John 9:7

Waters from the Spring of Gihon flow through Hezekiah's Tunnel and fill the Pool of Siloam where Jesus sent the blind man to wash.

Shakespeare's Juliet wasn't the first to wonder, "What's in a name?" Nor was she the last. Perhaps as you read about Jesus healing the man who was blind from birth, you, too, wonder, "What's in a name?"

Siloam means "sent," but the significance of the name is not easily grasped.

The water that fills the Pool of Siloam does not originate there. It is *sent* there by means of an underground passageway called Hezekiah's Tunnel. Cut through solid rock, it channels water from the Spring of Gihon on the other side of Mount Zion to this reservoir inside the walls of the ancient city of Jerusalem.

In Jesus' day, everyone knew this was a unique pool because it wasn't a cistern and it wasn't a spring. Its source was a hidden spring quite a distance away.

John called attention to the meaning of the word *Siloam* because he wanted to call attention to something of spiritual significance too. The pool called "Sent" was an appropriate place to send the blind man. And who sent him? The one who Himself was sent—Jesus, the one who said He was sent by God to do works of cleansing (9:4).

The blind man obeyed Jesus' command completely. He probably passed a dozen other places where he could have washed, but he continued on his way to the Pool of Siloam because that was where Jesus sent him.

Arriving at the pool, he groped his way to the edge, knelt down, scooped up a handful of water, and washed the dried, brown mud from his eyes. In that act of obedience he received his sight.

Think of it! A man who had known only darkness all his life now saw light! His eyes were opened. He was overwhelmed. He didn't really know Jesus; he didn't even know His name. But Jesus sent him and he obeyed.

The Father sent Jesus and He obeyed. He was sent for our cleansing.

The water is sent by way of the tunnel, and it flows to the place prepared for it.

The Lord sends you to do His will. You may not understand it now, but will you go? Will you obey?

Lord Jesus, you were sent for my cleansing, and you obediently came. The blind man was sent for his cleansing, and he obediently went. I also have been sent into my world. I will obediently heed your voice.

INSIGHT

Hezekiah's Tunnel is an amazing feat of ancient engineering dated to 700 B.C. Stonecutters, starting from opposite ends and chipping their way through 1770 feet (540 m) of solid rock, marvelously met in the middle of the tunnel.

A Hebrew inscription describing this achievement has been recovered from the tunnel wall. It reads: "The tunnel is completed. This is the story of the tunnel. While the stonecutters were lifting up the pick, each toward his neighbor (from the opposite ends), and while they were yet 3 cubits apart, there was heard a voice of one calling to another; and after that, pick struck against pick; and waters flowed from the Spring to the Pool, 1200 cubits and 100 cubits was the height of the rock above."

ENRICHMENT

Here is a truly unforgettable experience! The brave and daring are welcome to wade in the dark from one end of the tunnel to the other. Of course, this requires suitable shoes, clothing, and a flashlight, but it takes only about half an hour. The memories are guaranteed to last a lifetime.

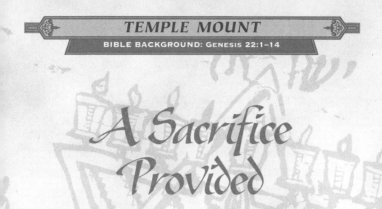

TEMPLE MOUNT

BIBLE BACKGROUND: GENESIS 22:1–14

A Sacrifice Provided

Abraham answered, "God himself will provide the lamb for the burnt offering, my son."

Genesis 22:8

The Dome of the Rock dominates the Temple Mount today, but the nearby El-Aqsa Mosque and Western Wall are also significant sites that draw worshipers and tourists to the same general area.

A sacrifice is not a sacrifice unless there is something to slay. Isaac knew that. So did Abraham. Yet their preparations for a sacrifice on Mount Moriah included everything except something to slay.

Finally Isaac asked his father the obvious: "The fire and the wood are here, but where is the lamb for the burnt offering?" And Abraham replied cryptically, "God himself will provide the lamb for the burnt offering, my son."

Was this a statement of Abraham's faith? Was it a prophecy about the future? Or was it a deliberately ambiguous reply meant to keep Isaac from probing further? Perhaps it was a combination of all of the above.

Certainly it was less than a direct response to Isaac's question. Perhaps Abraham sensed that his son was growing increasingly uneasy. As a young man, probably in his late teens, Isaac had witnessed many sacrifices. Maybe he had even taken similar journeys with his father before. Whatever his intent, Abraham did not disclose that Isaac himself was the intended sacrifice.

Abraham the patriarch was also Abraham the prophet (Genesis 20:7). He stood in a unique position before God. Sometimes God gave him special abilities to foretell the future. His statement here was a prediction of the coming of Christ. Though Abraham could not comprehend the full meaning of his prophecy, later generations would. When John the Baptist saw Jesus at the Jordan he declared, "Look, the Lamb of God, who takes away the sin of the world!" (John 1:29).

Abraham's enigmatic reply to Isaac was also a statement of his unflinching faith. He knew what God had commanded, and he believed that God would provide the means necessary to carry it out. Even without full understanding, there was full faith. As the writer to the Hebrews explained centuries later, "Abraham reasoned that God could raise the dead . . ." (Hebrews 11:19).

God vindicated Abraham's faith. For the immediate sacrifice, he provided a ram as a substitution for Isaac.

For the ultimate sacrifice, He provided His own Son as a substitution for us. As proof of His right to require the incomprehensible and His ability to respond with the miraculous, God provided the resurrection of His own Son from the dead.

Heavenly Father, you have provided for me a perfect sacrifice by giving me your Son Jesus to die in my place. May I faithfully give to you all that you ask, believing you are able to provide.

INSIGHT

The word *Moriah* is a play on words that means "the place where God provides." It is used only twice in Scripture. In Genesis 22:2, it denotes the region where Abraham was told to go to sacrifice Isaac. In 2 Chronicles 3:1, Mount Moriah is the specific hill where Solomon built his temple.

Beneath the shining Dome of the Rock is a large stone that many Jews and Christians identify as the place where Abraham prepared to sacrifice Isaac. There is no archeological evidence to prove that this is the site where God provided a ram in place of Isaac. Channels cut into this rock, however, would seem to indicate it was used at some point in history as an altar for regular animal sacrifices.

The nearby western retaining wall of Herod's Temple proves that this is the general location of Solomon's Temple as well. This rock, which is 59 x 43 feet (18 x 13 m), must have been incorporated into the temple or its complex.

ENRICHMENT

For many Christians, sensing God's presence on the Temple Mount is an enormous challenge. It is not that God isn't there; He is present everywhere. But present also on the Temple Mount today is the pervasive presence of Islam, embodied in the imposing Dome of the Rock.

Inside this blue-walled, gold-domed shrine is "the Rock." Not only is it known to Christians and Jews as the place of Abraham's altar for the sacrifice of Isaac and as the location of Solomon's temple, "the Rock" is also revered by the Muslims as the spot from which the prophet Mohammed ascended on horseback straight into heaven.

Because this is a Muslim place of worship, with Arabic music and prayers echoing constantly, Christians can find it difficult to worship here. Nonetheless, prayer is needed. This is a perfect place to ask God to shine His light into darkened hearts, as 2 Corinthians 4:4 suggests. "The god of this age has blinded the minds of unbelievers, so that they cannot see the light of the gospel of the glory of Christ, who is the image of God."

Enter With Thanksgiving

Enter his gates with thanksgiving and his courts with praise; give thanks to him and praise his name.

Psalm 100:4

Jesus Himself ascended these ancient steps cut from bedrock on the south side of Temple Mount.

There are only a few locations where one can stand and say with certainty, "Jesus walked here." The massive steps on the south side of the Temple Mount provide one such inspiring place.

Excavations following the 1967 War uncovered a long and imposing stairway leading to the top of the Temple Mount. Because these steps are cut from bedrock, there is no doubt that they are the very ones Jesus trod on His many visits to the Temple.

At the top of the stairs in the far west corner, a piece of carved archway protrudes from the wall. Scholars identify this as part of one of the Hulda gates, through which worshipers passed as they ascended the Temple Mount.

As the devout advanced on their way to worship, they customarily sang a song of praise. The well-known one-hundredth Psalm may have been on the adoring lips of thousands as they climbed these stairs, singing, "Enter his gates with thanksgiving and his courts with praise; give thanks to him and praise his name."

Today, God still wants His children to approach His throne with an attitude of gratitude. He wants to hear our praises before we burst into petition. He wants to know we love and appreciate Him for what He means *to* us as much as what He can do *for* us.

The psalmist provides the joyful worshiper with several reasons for praise. The Lord is our Creator-God. He provides security and significance for all who are His, like a good shepherd caring for his sheep. Yes, our God is truly good. His covenant love is steadfast and sure. Let there be no doubt about His faithfulness for all who come to Him.

Perhaps Jesus Himself intoned this psalm of thanksgiving to the Father as He ascended these ancient steps. Let all God's children lift their voices in joyful songs of praise.

My heart overflows with thanksgiving to you, O God. May I sing your praises throughout all my days.

INSIGHT

As many large churches have discovered, accommodating thousands of worshipers requires a method of regulating traffic flow. Apparently the Temple at Jerusalem had its own system. What is today called Wilson's Arch supported a bridge from the upper city to the west side of the Temple Mount. Robinson's Arch, located at the southwest corner of the Temple Mount, is thought to have supported a stairway down to street level. When worshipers used the Hulda gates on the Temple Mount's south side, they likely entered the gate from the east and exited through the one on the west.

ENRICHMENT

While seated on the Temple's ancient bedrock steps, your group could hold a testimony service. The one hundredth Psalm provides the inspiration for your praises. There is no better place in all the world to make a joyful noise unto the Lord.

Good Advice

Observe what the Lord your God requires: Walk in his ways, and keep his decrees and commands, his laws and requirements, as written in the Law of Moses, so that you may prosper in all you do and wherever you go.

1 Kings 2:3

An orthodox Jew with phylacteries on his arms and forehead prays at the site of King David's Tomb.

The value of advice is measured by the experience behind it. We do well to accept the counsel of those who prove by their experience that they know what they are talking about. But we are wise to reject the directives of people whose lives do not match what they say.

Near the end of his life, King David offered Solomon, his son and chosen heir to the throne, some simple straightforward advice. He told him how to run his life and manage the kingdom. David knew what it took to be a good ruler because forty years had taught him some weighty lessons.

First, it is better to please God than people. The pressures on a leader were intense. The crowds clamored from every corner asking for special favors. Trusted advisors whispered their personal agendas at every opportunity. But doing what God required was the leader's paramount responsibility.

Second, God's ways are revealed in God's Word. David pointed his son to the Scriptures as his source of direction. His words reflected the charge found in Deuteronomy 17:18-19. The new king must "write for himself on a scroll a copy of this law . . . . It is to be with him, and he is to read it all the days of his life so that he may learn to revere the Lord his God and follow carefully all the words of this law and these decrees."

Third, walking with God brings blessing. David had felt the smile of God lighting his life, perhaps more than any other king of Israel. He was the one known as "a man after God's own heart." While he was not perfect, he had always returned to the true path whenever he had wandered.

Last, going astray has consequences. When David sinned with Bathsheba and ordered Uriah's death, the consequences were severe. The innocent suffered, his leadership lagged, and his heart was broken.

All this he wished to communicate to Solomon. His advice was good because he was a veteran of life, love, and leadership. If only his son would be wise enough to profit from the experiences of his father. If only we would join him.

Good advice—we all need it. Only the wise heed it.

Lord, teach me to measure the value of advice by the kind of life behind it. May I be wise enough to listen when the voice of experience speaks.

A large, stone cenotaph draped with rich embroidered fabric marks the traditional site of the Tomb of King David. This massive tomb-marker, however, is not his actual grave. His bones do not rest here.

First Kings 2:10 says Israel's greatest king was buried in the City of David, which is east of Mount Zion. The present site was not hallowed until about the fourth or fifth century A.D. The ancient stone walls that surround the monument to King David are considered part of the oldest synagogue yet discovered in Jerusalem. Here the faithful have come for centuries. In fact, before the Western Wall was accessible, this was a favorite place for committed Jews to pray and seek God's face.

ENRICHMENT

The Tomb of King David is still a sanctified spot for prayer. Dedicated worshipers with their scull caps and phylacteries come here often to read the Scriptures and pray aloud. Pause long enough to add your voice to the echoes of this tiny room.

Food for Thought

For who is greater, the one who is at the table or the one who serves? Is it not the one who is at the table? But I am among you as one who serves.

Luke 22:27

The beautiful, classic architecture of the place identified as the Upper Room belies any claim to authenticity as the site of the Last Supper.

So often family food times turn into family feud times. When everyone sits down for a meal, the conversation is not always sweet. Sometimes it turns sour, and arguments erupt. If this happens in your home, don't think it unique. It happened even during Jesus' last meal with His disciples.

Although all four gospels tell of the Last Supper, only Luke recorded the quarrel among the apostles. It was the disciples' dispute over who was greatest that provoked Jesus to get up, gird Himself with a towel, and wash their feet. While John provided the text of that famous deed, it was Luke who supplied the context.

Jesus pointed His followers to three positive examples of servanthood.

The first was what Jesus referred to as "the youngest" (22:26). In the typical first-century family, the youngest had fewer rights and privileges than the eldest. Therefore, Jesus' command to be like the youngest was another way to say, "Don't worry about your rights. Just do what is right."

Next, Jesus drew attention to the one who serves. A servant, simply defined, is one who helps others. If we have a position of authority, it is a God-given opportunity to serve others. In Christ's kingdom, those who rule have a mandate to minister.

Christ concluded His supper-time sermon by focusing on the final and strongest example of servanthood—Himself. He reminded His followers, "I am among you as one who serves." For thirty years He had served His family. For three years, He had served the sick, the blind, the hungry, and the demon-possessed. In the next few hours, He served the entire human race by sacrificing His life for their sin.

The lesson of service is not easily learned. Even at the Last Supper, the disciples needed to learn it. Today our Lord continues to instruct His followers in the art of serving others.

Dear Jesus, I am just like the disciples—slow to learn the lesson of servanthood. Don't give up on me. Your example inspires me to keep on growing.

INSIGHT

The traditional site where Jesus observed the Passover with His disciples, is called the Upper Room or the Cenacle (meaning dining room). The vaulted hall is impressive but certainly not authentic. It wasn't built until the fourteenth century A.D.

Even the location must be suspect since it is situated over the traditional site of King David's Tomb. People just do not build houses over kings' tombs. Even if they did, the Jewish historian Josephus tells us that David's tomb was marked by a huge monument.

Regardless, a serious student does not need the Upper Room in order to learn the lesson of servanthood. Service can be learned in one's own dining room, or kitchen, or classroom, or office, or church, or anywhere God has placed him or her.

ENRICHMENT

As you stand in the great hall that tradition has labeled the Upper Room, imagine your family eating supper here with Jesus. How do you feel? What will you do?

Perhaps you have begun to experience closer relationships with people in your group. Those who were once just strangers have become almost like family. How would Jesus have you serve them today?

Way of Sorrows

He was despised and rejected by men, a man of sorrows, and familiar with suffering.

Isaiah 53:3

Today tourists and locals rub shoulders as they travel down the Via Dolorosa, the course that tradition says Jesus walked on the way to the cross.

Life's heaviest burdens are not weighed in pounds. Rather, they are measured by mental anguish and marked by emotional distress. The sense of sin, the weight of wrongdoing, the gravity of guilt—these are life's truly heavy loads.

But how much does the wickedness of the whole world weigh? How heavy are the sins of the entire human race? These were the burdens Jesus bore as He stumbled down the "Way of Sorrows" toward Calvary.

Amazingly, the gospel writers did not dwell on the depth of Jesus' suffering. They avoided sensationalism and downplayed the details. They told us nothing of Jesus' feelings. They stuck strictly to the facts. Even the awful act of crucifixion was reported with stark simplicity: "Here they crucified him."

Yet certainly, sin-caused sorrow is the heaviest burden Christ carried to Calvary. His wooden cross had been lifted by Simon the Cyrene. He persevered under what the prophet Isaiah pointed out as *our* infirmities, *our* sorrows, *our* transgressions, *our* iniquities.

That was the greatest weight. Tradition tells us it pushed Him to the pavement more than once. The bleeding shoulders of Jesus carried the sins of the world to Calvary. There His mission was completed and our guilt was removed.

Lord Jesus Christ, my many sins increased your sorrows. Your suffering removed my guilt. May I learn to live in the freedom, grace, and gratitude you came to give.

INSIGHT

The Via Dolorosa commemorates the path of Jesus' Passion, leading from Pilate's judgment hall to Golgotha. However, the exact route He traveled through the streets of Jerusalem is not clear. There are two major uncertainties.

First, we do not know for sure where the stone pavement (Greek *Lithostrotos*) named in John 19:13 is located. Many scholars agree it is likely at the site of the Fortress of Antonia. If so, it is now found in the basement of the Church of the Sisters of Zion.

This 2500 square-yard (2000 square-m) area is paved with hard limestone blocks 1 yard square and 1 foot thick (1 m square and 30 cm thick). Etched in these stones you can see geometric designs that, apparently, were games played by the Roman soldiers.

Above the place of the pavement stands the Ecce Homo Arch. *Ecce Homo* is Latin for "this man," which is translated as "Here is the man!" in John 19:5. These were Pilate's famous words as he displayed the bruised and beaten Christ to the clamoring crowd outside his judgment hall.

The present-day Ecce Homo Arch can be viewed on the traditional Via Dolorosa. Archeologists tell us that this arch was actually built after the time of Christ and was part of the northeast entrance gate to Jerusalem that Hadrian built during his reign, A.D. 117–138. Although it is not the precise place, it does most likely stand near the spot.

The second problem with exact identification of the Via Dolorosa is the location of Golgotha (see p. 36).

The traditional route of Christ's sorrow is an east to west route from the Lions' Gate (or Fortress of Antonia) to the Church of the Holy Sepulchre, a distance of about half a mile (.8 km). Along this route are the fourteen stations of the cross, with the final five being inside the Church itself. Your guide can point out the sculptured relief forms in the walls and columns along the way. Without this expert help, they are easily missed.

ENRICHMENT

There are very few places in the Holy Land where you can say with certainty, "I walked today where Jesus walked." Even the route of the Via Dolorosa is disputed. And to be honest, the street the tourist treads is several feet higher than the level where Jesus walked. But there is one point along the Via Dolorosa where some first-century paving stones can be seen. It is in the middle of a busy intersection. Ask your guide to point it out. Stand there, if only for the briefest moment, and capture the sights, sounds, and smells around you. Treasure that moment and take it home.

Pray for Peace

Pray for the peace of Jerusalem: "May those who love you be secure. May there be peace within your walls and security within your citadels."

Psalm 122:6–7

An orthodox Jew reads the Torah at the foot of the Western Wall.

There is nothing like the experience of praying at the Western Wall of the Temple Mount in Jerusalem. Here the faithful gather from all over the world to lift their petitions to Almighty God. Many write their prayers on slips of paper and stuff them in the cracks of the wall.

Faithful Jews have come for years to the Western Wall mourning the loss of the Temple in A.D. 70. Here, too,

Christians come to pray. They pray for the day the temple will be rebuilt. They know that the rebuilding of the temple will signal the return of the Lord. His second coming in power and glory is the longing of every believer.

Here people pray for all manner of personal concerns. This place inspires no small prayers. It evokes from human hearts the deepest yearnings and highest hopes. Passionate tears drip down faces of devoted disciples who long to reach the throne of God while standing by these stones.

Here, too, they pray for the peace of Jerusalem. Such peace has never been more necessary, yet it has never been more elusive. Arab-Israeli hostilities are constant. The Dome of the Rock, looming just over the Western Wall, represents ever-present religious conflict. Political peace is fragile at best. The peace that this nation needs cannot be forged by human leaders alone. Divine intervention is necessary, and only prayer can bring it about.

"Pray for the peace of Jerusalem"—this is the charge God has issued to His people of all generations. May the Prince of Peace bring His everlasting peace to this land.

Prince of Peace, bring your peace to those who love this holy city. You alone can transform the hearts and minds of people caught in hatred, prejudice, and confusion.

INSIGHT

What makes this such a special place to pray?

First of all, it is ancient and authentic. These timeworn stones compose part of the west retaining wall of the Temple Mount. Beginning in 20 B.C. Herod the Great worked until his death to enlarge and reconstruct the Temple and the surrounding area. The public prayer area, which is all that most tourists see, represents only 10 percent of recent excavations. A tunnel now extends an additional 800 feet (250 m) along the wall and under the buildings to the north. These excavations prove this site is the actual location of the Temple where Jesus worshiped.

Second, this wall is awesome. Although it rises nearly 50 feet (15 m) high, it also extends another 52 feet (16 m) below the ground level of the public plaza. Joined without mortar, many of its hand-hewn limestone blocks display the characteristic Herodian margin around their weathered faces.

Finally, this wall is all that is known to remain of the holiest place in all Israel, the ancient Temple Mount. God promised that his presence would dwell in the Temple's holy of holies. Yet the Temple Mount itself is occupied

now by the Dome of the Rock and other Moslem shrines. Therefore, for observant Jews, the Western Wall is the closest they are permitted to come to their most revered holy place.

As Israeli soldiers look south from their guard station they see the Western Wall of the Temple dividing the Jews praying at the plaza (right) from the Muslims worshiping atop the Temple Mount (left).

ENRICHMENT

You may stand at this holy place only once in your life. What will you pray for? Write your prayer on a small piece of paper. Voice your petitions to God, then add your prayer to the thousands already crammed in the crannies of this historic wall.

Men who visit the Western Wall must have their heads covered. If you have your own yarmulke, be sure to take it along. If not, you will have to use the paper ones provided.

Digging for Truth

Jesus answered them, "Destroy this temple, and I will raise it again in three days."

John 2:19

A sense of history penetrates the minds of travelers along the Western Wall Tunnel.

Theology is like archeology. What you see on the surface isn't all there is. If you want the good stuff, you've got to dig deeper.

Because the unbelieving Jews weren't willing to dig deeper, they missed the true meaning of Jesus' statement about the Temple. They knew it had taken King Herod's workforce 46 years to construct this magnificent edifice. They saw its dimensions. They considered the massive size of the building blocks. They quickly concluded, "No way!"

On the surface, they were right. It would be impossible to reconstruct the Temple in such a short time. Excavations in the Western Wall Tunnel confirm such a conclusion. In a section of the Temple Mount retaining wall referred to as the Master Course, there is one stone that by itself is calculated to weigh 600 tons (550 metric tons)! No wonder the Jews decided Jesus' prediction to rebuild the Temple was an architectural absurdity.

But Jesus wasn't talking about architecture. The temple He referred to was His physical body. Destroy it, and He would raise it to life again on the third day. This was a theological prophecy of infinite dimensions.

Jesus was declaring that His death and resurrection would be the foundation for a new order of worship and a higher kind of life. But everyone, including His disciples, missed the real meaning of His statement. What they perceived on the surface didn't make sense, and they failed to explore any further.

Sometimes we are guilty of the same error. We miss the richer revelations of Scripture because our quiet time is too short. A rapid reading of the text is insufficient for complete understanding. However, by using just three elementary Bible study tools, we can discover so much more.

First, alternate Bible versions allow us to compare our favorite translation with others. Sometimes a paraphrase can bring familiar passages to life. Contemporary wording may offer a fresh viewpoint on verses we have read a hundred times. Even if we don't agree with the writer's interpretation, it can serve to break up our caked and crusty thinking.

Second, a Bible concordance can lead us to new veins of truth that run parallel to the passage at hand. We can look up key words and trace their usage in other places. Take faith and works, for example. The relationship between these two concepts is discussed by both James and the Apostle Paul. By comparing the different writers' perspectives, we are able to better understand the interactive role of faith and works in the Christian's life.

Third, commentaries by pastors and other Bible scholars are valuable. They supply historical background that brings new dimension to the pages of Scripture. Their suggestions for personal application can help the hearer of the Word become a doer of the Word.

The infinite treasures of Scripture can never be exhausted. With just a few simple tools the dedicated Bible explorer can turn up more truth. Great discoveries lie in store for each one who is willing to dig a little deeper.

Lord Jesus, I confess that I often miss much of the meaning in your Word because I only skim the surface. I want to dig deeper. Reward my efforts with the joy of discovery.

INSIGHT

Laid end-to-end the four huge stones that comprise the Master Course stretch more than 100 feet (30 m). The largest is 11 feet high, 42 feet long, and an estimated 14 feet wide (3.5 m x 13 m x 4 m). One may rightly wonder how the builders were able to set such huge stones into place on the wall. While no one can be certain of details, at least part of the answer is that the massive stone blocks were lowered into place, not raised. Working with gravity, rather than against it, made the task much simpler.

The quarry for these stones is at the north end of the wall, and it is higher than this course of the wall. Nevertheless, even with ropes and pulleys, the task was still a major engineering feat.

ENRICHMENT

The tunnel is an impressive place, and the Master Course is especially awesome. The engineering genius of the ancients is marvelous. Yet such skill and ability is nothing compared to the miraculous power of God. He can raise the dead! In the semi-darkness of the tunnel, take a moment to thank God for His "incomparably great power for us who believe. That power is like the working of his mighty strength, which he exerted in Christ when he raised him from the dead" (Ephesians 1:19-20).

Judea
&
Samaria

Friendship With Unbelievers

So that place was called Beersheba, because the two men swore an oath there.

Genesis 21:31

Excitement swirls around the open-air market in Beersheba as merchants offer their wares to townspeople and tourists.

The Bible declares that anyone who is a friend of the world is an enemy of God. Yet Abraham, who was known as the friend of God, was also the covenant friend of Abimelech, an unbeliever. It is possible for mature

Christians to form friendships with unbelievers and honor God in the process.

The friendship between these two great men began because of God's bountiful blessing on Abraham. In the words of Abimelech, king of Gerar, "God is with you in everything you do." The king's first encounter with the patriarch taught him that Abraham was not perfect (Genesis 20). Yet God's blessing was so undeniable that Abimelech was compelled to seek a relationship with him. Abimelech took the initiative, and Abraham showed no hesitation in responding.

Abraham had learned a lesson from his previous duplicity and decided that honesty was truly the best policy. So, rather than ignore a recent dispute over the ownership of a well, Abraham brought up the subject immediately. To do so risked the wrath of this powerful leader. (Ironically, fear of the king's wrath had prompted Abraham's previous deception.) Abimelech, however, was quick to resolve the matter and acknowledged that the well belonged to Abraham. No doubt, their friendship was helped by their mutual honesty.

Also, the relationship between these two great men and their descendants was perpetuated by a promise. While Abimelech seemed unfamiliar with Abraham's covenant customs, he readily accepted the seven lambs as assurance of the treaty he sought. Thus the place of the promise was named Beersheba, "Well of Seven."

Here two great men, one the founder of the household of faith, the other a prominent unbeliever, established a long-lasting friendship. God's blessing on the man of faith drew them together. Mutual honesty advanced their alliance. A promise preserved it for many generations to come.

Lord Jesus, you were known as a friend of sinners. Grant me the wisdom and grace to know how to establish friendships with unbelievers that will honor your name and advance your purposes.

The biblical phrase "from Dan to Beersheba" acknowledged Beersheba as the southernmost point on the ancient map of the Promised Land. Today this modern city serves as the capital of the Negev and the hub of all activity in the south. Located 48 miles (77 km) southwest of Jerusalem, it is already Israel's fourth-largest city and is growing rapidly.

An odd, wooden, wheel-like structure known as Abraham's Well is a must-see for tourists, though in actuality, it has no known connection with the patriarch. Evidences of several wells, however, have been discovered in the area, the largest being more than 12 feet (3.5 m) in diameter and cut through solid rock.

ENRICHMENT

If you venture to Beersheba try to visit on a Thursday morning when the Bedouin market unfurls its colors and spreads its wares. You can barter for bargains of boundless variety amidst a Middle Eastern kaleidoscope of intriguing sights, sounds, and smells.

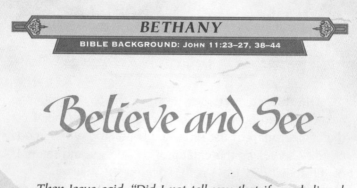

Believe and See

Then Jesus said, "Did I not tell you that if you believed, you would see the glory of God?"

John 11:40

The Tomb of Lazarus in Bethany affords the adventurous traveler an opportunity to descend into the heart of a typical first-century cave-tomb.

Some things have to be believed to be seen. That is why Jesus raised Lazarus from the dead. He performed one last crowning miracle to spark the faith of all those watching. And He called upon their faith and participation to make the miracle happen.

Miracles first require a firm faith in who Jesus is. When Jesus spoke to Lazarus' sister Martha, He challenged her to declare her faith. Her confession of faith was clear and strong: "Yes, Lord," she told Him, "I believe that you are the Christ, the Son of God, who was to come into the world" (11:27).

Second, miracles take a faith that is willing to obey, even without complete understanding. When Jesus commanded that the stone over the tomb entrance be removed, He met with objection. Even Martha, who had just affirmed Jesus' lordship, reemphasized the facts of Lazarus' death.

Patiently, Jesus reminded her again that she needed to trust Him and believe. "Did I not tell you that if you believed, you would see the glory of God?" (11:40). The glorious miracles of God are experienced by those whose belief is practical and not merely theological.

Jesus required that people get involved in making the miracle happen. He asked them to remove the stone. Although He could have removed it miraculously, He knew it was better for them to participate. Their obedience proved their faith.

Similarly, when Lazarus came out of the tomb, he was still wrapped in tight burial cloths. Instead of releasing the cloths miraculously, Jesus commanded others to remove them. Their actions cemented their beliefs. Their testimony was stronger because they had a part in the fulfillment of the miracle.

Maybe you need a miracle in your life today. Remember, miracles require faith on the front end. While it is easier to believe *after* you have seen, some things have to be believed *before* they can be seen.

Lord, I believe you are the Christ, the Son of God, who has come into the world. I believe that nothing is too difficult for you. Grant me faith to believe so that I may see the glory of God revealed in my circumstances.

A chapel was built over the supposed location of Lazarus' tomb in the late fourth century. However, there is no archeological evidence to prove this site is authentic.

The gospel writer tells us Lazarus' tomb was a cave (John 11:38). Once inside the tomb that today bears an official-looking marker, the visitor discovers a two-chambered tomb—a vestibule and a small inner chamber. The inner chamber has three raised burial niches.

Perhaps this is the tomb of Lazarus, but probably not. The best we can say is that it is a typical cave tomb located in Bethany. As Christians, we can be assured of the miracle without being certain of the site.

ENRICHMENT

If you are on the lookout for unique and inexpensive souvenirs, Bethany has something special to offer. Near the Tomb of Lazarus, you can purchase a hand-woven slingshot similar to the one David might have used to slay Goliath. (It is uncertain why these are only sold here, as Bethany has no known connection to King David.) Nonetheless, along with five smooth stones from the Valley of Elah, a slingshot makes a great object lesson.

Bethlehem's Surprise!

While they were there, the time came for the baby to be born, and she gave birth to her firstborn, a son. She wrapped him in cloths and placed him in a manger, because there was no room for them in the inn.

Luke 2:6–7

The fourteen-point silver star in the Grotto of the Nativity marks the spot where millions of pilgrims have paused to remember the birth of Christ.

The birth of Jesus is one of the most familiar stories of Christianity, yet it is full of surprises.

One of the first surprises came to Joseph. Surely he must have been shocked to be visited by an angel. But when he learned that his beloved was already pregnant with a child that he knew was not his own, he was over-whelmed. When the census-taking required that he and Mary travel to his hometown of Bethlehem, Joseph logically expected to find a place to stay with his family or friends. Yet, when they arrived, the only accommodation available was a stable.

Undoubtedly the circumstances of Jesus' birth were not what Mary had imagined either. Most likely she pictured herself giving birth in a welcoming family setting. At the least she anticipated a clean bed and a warm blanket. She must have looked forward to being attended by other women experienced in these matters. Instead, when the time came to deliver her child, Mary found herself on a cold floor, softened perhaps by a bit of clean straw, and attended only by her husband.

Even the shepherds were startled by the circumstances of the Messiah's birth. They weren't looking for a serenade from a choir of angels when they settled down to watch their flocks that first Christmas night. The glory of the Lord that shone around them struck terror in their hearts. The news that they would find their Savior lying in a common feeding trough for animals was simply too incredible. They had to run to Bethlehem to see if it all were true.

The King of the universe entered our world in an amazing manner. He left the glory of the eternal throne of God to be born in a dirty stable. He turned His back to the perfections of heaven and opened His eyes to a world of sin.

The only one not surprised by this humble Bethlehem birth was Jesus Himself. He had had it planned for ages. He chose it. It was the first step of His journey to the cross where He would give His life for us.

That is the real surprise of Bethlehem.

Thank you, Jesus, for your willingness to enter my world through Bethlehem's stable door. Your amazing humility is the beginning of my salvation.

Bethlehem still holds surprises. The concept of Jesus' being born in a cave is new to many. Having seen hundreds of Christmas cards, Sunday school pictures, and wooden nativity scenes, we have come to accept such interpretations as fact. Yet the strength of tradition and the evidence of history indicate that it is more likely that Christ was born in a cave than in an open-air shed.

The once plain and simple grotto over which the Church of the Nativity is built has been dramatically altered and decorated. Its marble floor and tapestry-draped walls disguise the rough and crude surroundings that Jesus' eyes first saw. Built into the wall, and looking much like a fireplace with the grate removed, is a marble-faced structure. On the floor is a large silver star said to mark the spot where Jesus was born. Many an unsuspecting pilgrim has found the visit to Bethlehem a big surprise.

ENRICHMENT

To reach the Church of the Nativity you must cross a broad plaza that often is busy with merchants hawking their wares. Bypass the hustle and bustle and go straight to the door of the church. Once inside, spend a few moments off to the side in private preparation before you descend to the grotto. Because of the volume of pilgrims who stream through this place each year, you may be allowed only a few moments in the cave itself.

Giving Means Living

Some give freely, yet grow all the richer; others withhold what is due, and only suffer want.

Proverbs 11:24 (NRSV)

The Dead Sea's high mineral content makes floating as relaxing as reading the morning paper.

Seven million tons of fresh water rush into the Dead Sea every day, but the sea never becomes fresher. The water just becomes stagnant. Because it only takes and never gives, the Dead Sea is a lake of liquid death.

It is the same way with people. Unless we pass along the blessings God gives us, we stagnate and die. Keeping it all for ourselves ends in disaster.

On the other hand, giving means living. When Jesus said, "It is more blessed to give than to receive," He might have illustrated it with a comparison of the Sea of Galilee and the Dead Sea. The Sea of Galilee is only one-fourth the size of its neighbor to the south, but it teems with life. It harbors nearly two dozen types of fish, irrigates hundreds of acres of crops, and supports the life of millions around it. The secret is that Galilee is nourished by the Jordan from the north, and yet it supplies its living waters to the Jordan at its southern outlet.

By contrast, the Dead Sea cannot support any kind of life—hence its name. No fish live in its waters except at the very mouth of the streams. It is useless for irrigation. Comparatively few settlements have existed on its shores, and, of course, even those were dependent upon freshwater springs and streams.

Like the Sea of Galilee, some people give freely, yet they gain even more. They are channels for God's blessings and resources. Their giving creates a capacity to receive more. They stay fresh, and they are a source of refreshment to others. Giving keeps them living.

Other people withhold what God intends for them to pass along. Instead of being a channel of blessing, they build a dam and become a stagnant pool. God's goodness gets clogged in the system.

God wants His blessings to us to be passed on through us. By giving we keep on living.

Dear God, I don't want to be like the Dead Sea! Help me to give cheerfully, confident of your endless supply. Make me a channel of your blessings and a source of refreshment to those around me.

While the Dead Sea cannot support life, it is not totally useless. For centuries it has provided salt to local and distant markets. Today commercial extraction of minerals is extensive in the southern third of the sea where the concentration of dissolved mineral solids is as high as thirty percent. Its murky waters yield calcium, sodium, and potassium for a variety of agricultural and industrial purposes.

The Dead Sea is doubly distinctive. It is the saltiest body of water anywhere. And it is the lowest place on the earth's surface, being 1306 feet (398 m) below sea level. When you have visited the Dead Sea, you have experienced one of the world's truly unique places.

ENRICHMENT

Death stinks. So does the Dead Sea. As you descend into the valley you may notice a nauseous smell. It is bromine, sulfur, and the evaporation of mineral salts. Should you inadvertently taste these greenish, oily waters you will find they are extremely bitter.

Floating in the Dead Sea is an unforgettable experience. Besides your swim suit and towel, you may want a pair of old sneakers or sandals for wearing between the bathhouse and the shore. The rocks get hot in the heat, which can soar above 100° Fahrenheit.

Pose your friends for a unique snapshot. Photograph them floating on their backs, hands and feet in the air, reading the morning newspaper.

Humility's Place

He must become greater; I must become less.

John 3:30

Ein Karem, the village identified as the birthplace of John the Baptist, lies nestled in the Judean hills west of Jerusalem.

John the Baptist was bold, brash, assertive, loud, frank, and strong. Ironically, he was also humble. Set amongst this audacious mix of personality traits, humility is even more noteworthy. Although John's disciples interpreted Jesus' growing popularity as spiritual competition, John saw it differently. His heart-response defines humility.

Humility recognizes God's sovereignty in all things. John reminded his followers that we can receive only what

God chooses to give (3:27). The Lord is ultimately in control of our destiny. The ebb and flow of popularity, prominence, and even prosperity are all a part of His plan. We cannot force anything that God does not ordain. Recognizing God's sovereignty allows us to relax in the confidence that God has our times in His hand.

Humility rejoices to play the role God assigns. John saw himself as the friend who finds satisfaction in serving the interests of the bride and groom and not his own (3:28–29). His example encourages us to be content without attention. Accept the position that God assigns. Don't worry about top billing, just play the part well. Then we will be prepared for what comes next.

Humility returns all the glory to God. John spoke about Jesus saying, "He must become greater; I must become less" (3:30). This classic statement shines as the hallmark of the humble heart. It reflects a readiness to exalt Jesus and efface self. It recognizes that in the end, the preeminence of Christ and the glory of God are all that really matter.

Humility crowns the list of Christian virtues. As Augustine remarked, "Should you ask me what is the first thing in religion, I should reply that the first, second, and third thing therein is humility." It is the virtue that allowed John to accept second place behind Jesus.

Humility is elusive, but I continue to seek it, Lord. Help me to give it priority, so that you may receive the glory.

INSIGHT

Although the Bible never mentions Ein Karem, this village just west of Jerusalem hosts two churches associated with John the Baptist. Tradition dating to the fifth century A.D. points to a grotto now contained in the Church of St. John the Baptist as the place of his birth. Nearby the Church of the Visitation marks the site where John's parents, Zechariah and Elizabeth, lived when Mary, the mother of our Lord, visited them (Luke 1:39).

ENRICHMENT

It seems fitting that the village known as John the Baptist's birthplace is itself small, plain, and relatively uncelebrated. But if you go there, don't miss the opportunity to learn humility from yet another self-effacing follower of Christ—His mother. The words of the *Magnificat* are inscribed in forty-one languages in the courtyard of the Church of the Visitation. Mary marveled, "From now on all generations will call me blessed, for the Mighty One has done great things for me" (Luke 1:48–49).

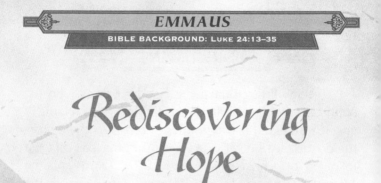

Rediscovering Hope

They asked each other, "Were not our hearts burning within us while he talked with us on the road and opened the Scriptures to us?"

Luke 24:32

The ruins of a Crusader church at a site about seventeen miles from Jerusalem provide a quiet place to reflect on one's personal walk with Christ. This site has much historical evidence in its favor.

"We had hoped" are three of the saddest words in the English language. They captured the total despair of the two disciples dragging themselves home to Emmaus after the death and resurrection of Jesus.

The past few days in Jerusalem had not been what they had anticipated. Jesus had not lived up to their expectations. They admitted, "We had hoped that he was the one who was going to redeem Israel" (24:21). More than that, they had hoped He would do it *their* way, on *their* timetable, and according to *their* idea of what was best.

With desires unfulfilled, they were not only discouraged about Jesus' death, they were even disappointed in the resurrection! They viewed the empty tomb as a reason for gloom rather than a cause for joy (24:22–24).

They did not understand that what they perceived as a setback was part of God's strategy to advance His plan for salvation. They failed to see the need for suffering on the road to redemption.

Their fog of disillusion prevented them from recognizing Jesus, even when He walked beside them. But Jesus penetrated their cloud of pessimism in two key ways.

First, He revealed Himself in the Scriptures. Though they had accepted many prophecies regarding the Messiah, they had stopped short of believing "all" that was foretold. Suffering simply did not fit into their scheme of salvation.

Next, Jesus revealed Himself in everyday circumstances. Once they studied the Scriptures carefully, they could understand life correctly. It was then that He sat down with them to a common, ordinary meal. And in the breaking of the bread, they recognized Him.

He had been with them all along. He was working His plan. He had brought redemption to Israel. But they could not see Him or comprehend His plan until they accepted all that the Scriptures taught.

We cannot understand life correctly until we grasp the complete message of the Bible. Life is full of change, disappointment, and puzzles. Not until we understand the Christ of Scripture can we begin to comprehend the meaning of our circumstances. But when we correctly understand God's plan as revealed in the Bible, then we can begin to comprehend His plan as it unfolds in our life.

Then understanding is gained. Joy is restored. And hope is rediscovered.

Lord Jesus Christ, I often fail to recognize your presence in my everyday circumstances. Perhaps it is because I still do not fully understand the principles you have placed in your Word. Open my eyes, and let me see you clearly.

INSIGHT

Locating the town of Emmaus is not as easy as you might think. A couple of problems complicate the process.

First, we do not know which direction it is from Jerusalem. Luke, the only New Testament writer to mention Emmaus, does not tell us.

Second, even the distance from Jerusalem is open to question. Although most modern translations indicate it is about 7 miles (11 km), there is another possibility. A few ancient manuscripts place it at 18 miles (30 km).

Because of this confusion, at least seven settlements have been proposed as possibilities for Emmaus. Current popular opinion seems to favor el Qubeibeh, 7 miles (11 km) northwest of Jerusalem. Roman, Crusader, and Byzantine ruins establish a political and religious presence in the area. Moreover, excavations in 1943 unearthed evidence of a first-century A.D. village nearby.

ENRICHMENT

An old Roman road near the village of el Qubeibeh may be the place where the risen Christ walked with His downhearted disciples. If your pilgrimage takes you to this town, don't miss the opportunity to shuffle down this dusty, tree-lined path. Can you sense the presence of the Lord? Can you hear Him whisper words of comfort to your heart?

Remnant of Rebellion?

He said to his men, "The Lord forbid that I should do such a thing to my master, the Lord's anointed, or lift my hand against him; for he is the anointed of the Lord."

1 Samuel 24:6

Ibex roam freely on the rocky hills of the En-Gedi Nature Reserve.

Clipping a corner of the king's robe was an act of rebellion. So when David cut off a piece of the royal robe it was a symbol of his ability to take the kingdom from King Saul.

The robe was a symbol of power. By his dress, Saul displayed his splendor and authority to everyone who saw him. Highly decorated, distinctively colored, and probably ornamented with gold threads, the king's robe was unique. As David showed off this royal remnant, he proved that the kingdom was within his grasp any time he wished to take it.

But how could this incident have taken place? Wouldn't it have been extremely difficult to get that close to the king without being detected? Consider these three factors.

First of all, we know the cave was deep (24:3). Either the king's men did not check the cave for the presence of enemies, or at least they did not check it thoroughly.

Also, the cave offered relief from the scorching temperatures of the En Gedi desert, west of the Dead Sea. When in public, the king was obligated to swelter under his royal trappings, despite the heat. But once inside the cave, he welcomed the opportunity to lay aside his outer robe and be refreshed by the relative coolness. David sneaked up to where the robe was laid, but not necessarily close to Saul himself.

Apparently the section David cut from Saul's robe was small enough not to be immediately noticed when the king again put on his robes in the cave's semidarkness.

Afterward, David was conscience-stricken—not because he had ruined a royal robe, but because he was ashamed of the emotions in his heart. He also understood his actions signified rebellion. So David publicly declared his allegiance to the king. He disavowed rebellion and reasserted devotion. "I was that close, but I didn't kill you! I only took a souvenir to prove my proximity."

People still wear robes of power today. They may not be literal robes, but they are the trappings and symbols of their authority. Whose robe is in your hand? Whose leadership are you under? You have a choice either to support or sabotage that leadership.

Be like David. When others push you to undermine the leader's authority, don't do it. Instead, demonstrate your devotion. Remain loyal to those God has placed over you. In due time, you will be rewarded.

Heavenly Father, your Son Jesus demonstrated submission to your will in His life and in His death. David also provides an example from which I can learn. Though it is often hard, teach me to be loyal to my leaders, so you can lift me up in due time.

INSIGHT

En Gedi is an oasis in the desert. Its crystal clear spring seems to spout from a limestone cliff and cascades into a pool below. In ancient times, grapes, dates, and balsam trees were grown here (see Song of Solomon 1:14). Now a kibbutz farms the land and harvests dates. In addition, the kibbutz receives some income from people who use it as a study and retreat center.

Excavations at this historic and biblical site reveal it was occupied by Amorites in the Chalcolithic period (4300–3300 B.C.). Evidence of various settlements throughout both Old Testament and New Testament times portrays a checkered history.

Perhaps one of the most fascinating discoveries is a watch tower ruin and vat where balsam oil, or balm, used to be made. This fragrant oil was used to anoint the kings of Israel more than two thousand years ago.

ENRICHMENT

En Gedi means "Spring of the Goat." It is most probably a reference to the ibex that still inhabit the area. In fact, today there is a wildlife sanctuary at En Gedi that preserves the Nubian ibex in its natural habitat.

A photograph of an ibex would be a special way to remember this spot and its spiritual lesson: Don't horn in on the authority of leaders God has placed over you.

Tombs and Testimonies

Then Abraham breathed his last and died at a good old age, an old man and full of years; and he was gathered to his people. His sons Isaac and Ishmael buried him in the cave of Machpelah near Mamre . . . .

Genesis 25:8–9

The Tomb of the Patriarchs' architecture makes it an imposing local landmark.

The tombs of great people have always drawn the curious and the committed. In Hebron lie the bones of the patriarchs and matriarchs whose lives inspire the faithful of three great religions. The Tomb of the

Patriarchs dominates not only the city landscape, but also the thoughts of thousands who consider this place Judaism's second holiest site.

While the structures seen by modern-day pilgrims are not the actual tombs of the patriarchs, it is likely that the site is authentically the cave of Machpelah. This holy place can spark thoughts of these great leaders and the testimony of their lives. Most notable is Abraham himself.

Abraham is regarded as the father of a new spiritual nation. His offspring became the people of Israel. His faith in the one true God set him apart from all those who worshiped many gods. Judaism, Islam, and Christianity, the three great monotheistic world religions, all trace their roots to Abraham. What a difference the faith of one person can make!

Abraham's obedience to God made him a faithful follower. At the divine command, he set off "to a place he would later receive as his inheritance . . . even though he did not know where he was going" (Hebrews 11:8). From Ur to Haran to Shechem to Bethel and eventually to Hebron—his journeys covered 175 years and thousands of miles. Each step took him down a path where God taught him lessons of greater faith and costlier obedience.

In all his wanderings Abraham learned to know God better and follow Him more closely; thus, he was called God's friend. This noble appellation was not earned quickly or easily, but certainly it is a title of high distinction. "God's friend" implies a familiarity and trust that can be gained only by years of yielding and long miles of maturing.

Father of a new nation, faithful follower, friend of God—this is the testimony that Abraham's tomb evokes. It is a testimony we esteem and emulate today. It is a kind of map and marker along our personal path of following God.

Although I feel unworthy to compare my spiritual walk with that of Abraham's, still his testimony is one I

wish to have. May I follow you all lifelong and leave a
legacy of friendship with God.

In January 1997, after years of negotiations, the Palestinians gained control over 80 percent of Hebron. Today the results of Palestinian control are not yet clear. As soon as travel to this city (approximately 23 miles [37 km] southwest of Jerusalem) is considered safe, thousands of long-denied pilgrims will visit.

Over the site purported to be the cave of Machpelah is built the Mosque of Abraham. Inside this two-thousand-year-old enclosure are the cenotaphs of Abraham, Sarah, Isaac, Rebekah, Jacob, and Leah. Just outside the southwest wall is the cenotaph labeled the Tomb of Joseph. These large, stone, box-like monuments are the focus of veneration for each of the seven notables whose actual graves are thought to lie in the caves beneath each site.

In Old Testament passages such as Genesis 23:2, Hebron is also called Kiriath Arba. The name means literally "City of Four" or "Fourfold City."

If you journey to the Tomb of the Patriarchs in Hebron, be sure to take a peek inside the cave below the building. There are two places where this may be possible. One is from the outside of the enclosure near the center of the southeast wall. The other is inside the Hall of Isaac just to the left of the entrance to the synagogue, between the tombs of Abraham and Sarah. Although you won't be able to see very much, it is thrilling to think that this is perhaps the cave in which Abraham was buried.

A third opening into the cave is in the Hall of Isaac along the inside of the southeast wall, just to the right of the carved wooden pulpit. This narrow slit in the floor is now covered with rugs. However, it was through this opening that Moshe Dayan lowered a young girl just after the 1967 Six Day War. Equipped with a camera, she found the cavern mostly bare.

Besides the Tomb of the Patriarchs, Hebron is famous also for its blown glass. All sorts of beautiful goblets, bowls, and vases are created in soft pastel patterns or in brilliant blue.

Tale of Two Kings

When Herod realized that he had been outwitted by the Magi, he was furious, and he gave orders to kill all the boys in Bethlehem and its vicinity who were two years old and under...

Matthew 2:16

The flat top of Herodium distinguishes it from other hills southeast of Bethlehem.

Charles Dickens opens *A Tale of Two Cities* with the classic line: "It was the best of times, it was the worst of times." That is what residents of Bethlehem might have said of the day when Jesus was born. Christ was announced as King of the Jews with tidings of peace and good will, but His nativity occasioned the death of innocent babies at the hand of Herod, the Roman-appointed king of the Jews.

Contrast these two kings. Herod the Great was an Idumean, not Jewish at all. Through scheming, he was proclaimed king of the Jews by Rome in 40 B.C. He jealously guarded this position of power. The Herodium, his fortress palace just beyond Bethlehem, provided a place to hide when political conditions weren't safe in Jerusalem. Through murder and intrigue, he retained his power. Although Herod was aging and sick when Jesus was born, he perceived the Holy Infant as a threat to his earthly throne. His resultant slaughter of innocent children (Matthew 2:16) snuffed out the lives of an estimated twenty to seventy male babies. During his lifetime, he murdered many others, including his wife, his sons, and forty-five members of the Sanhedrin. At the time of his death, Herod was feared, hated, and condemned by his subjects and family alike. His reign was the worst of times for all in Israel.

But for those who would recognize Jesus as their spiritual King, His nativity represented the best of times. Born of a devout Jewish mother and sent as God's anointed King of the Jews, Jesus brought salvation. He never sought acclaim but actively avoided those who wanted to bestow on Him an earthly title. He commanded His disciples not to use the sword, for His kingdom was not of this world. He never built a palace, never sat on a throne. Instead, He washed the feet of His followers, healed the sick, loved His enemies, and lifted up the helpless. Nonetheless, when He died He was publicly proclaimed as "King of the Jews" in three languages. Through His death He saved millions, and Jesus Christ is still loved, honored, and worshiped worldwide as the one true King of kings.

Two kings' paths crossed in Bethlehem. One, through his reign of terror, brought pain and suffering to many. Today his grave is lost beneath a monumental pile of dust, and his soul is tormented in hell. The other, though born in a stable and shamefully crucified, now reigns forever in heaven. For those who bow to Him, it remains the best of times.

Jesus Christ, I acknowledge you as the great King of kings. You are my Lord and Savior. I give allegiance to you alone.

INSIGHT

The Herodium looks like a volcano pushed up from the floor of the Judean wilderness southeast of Bethlehem about 7 miles (11 km). Herod the Great built this fortress in 37 B.C. He created this flat-topped citadel by leveling the summit of the cone-shaped mound and ringing it with high walls and four round towers. Inside the fortified crater, he dug out huge cisterns and constructed a luxurious palace, a Roman bath house, and a synagogue. Although history records that Herod the Great was buried here, his grave has not been discovered.

ENRICHMENT

After ascending the two hundred white marble steps leading to the summit of the Herodium, catch your breath and take in the view. This magnificent panorama looks out over Bethlehem and the Judean hills. Face Bethlehem and pause for a few moments to worship the King of kings who sits enthroned forever (Psalm 102:12).

Rescue the Perishing

But a Samaritan, as he traveled, came where the man was; and when he saw him, he took pity on him.

Luke 10:33

The Inn of the Good Samaritan sits beside the old Roman Road going down to Jericho from Jerusalem.

The road from Jerusalem to Jericho was a place where blood often flowed. It was known as the "Bloody Way," perhaps because travelers there were often beaten and robbed. Even into the twentieth century it was a place to avoid on a dark night.

Jesus set His parable of the Good Samaritan on this Roman road because His listeners knew its reputation. From Jerusalem to Jericho, the road dropped nearly 3500 feet (1.2 km) in less than twenty-five miles (32 km). Its steep descent wound through rocky and rugged territory, where only the rough and rowdy lived. Its caves and hollows made ideal hideouts for bandits and bums.

The plight of the traveler in Jesus' story was predictable. He lost his money, his goods, his donkey, his clothes, and nearly his life. Utterly helpless, he was left to die alongside the road.

A priest saw him but crossed to the other side without getting involved. Maybe he was on his way home from service at the temple. Perhaps he reasoned that he had been separated from his family for a long time, and they were expecting him.

A Levite, a priest's helper, followed the example of the religious leader. He saw the broken man but ignored his need.

Then a Samaritan, despised by the Jews, saw the wounded man and responded with compassion. Without hesitation, he rolled up his sleeves and began to help.

The Good Samaritan risked his own life knowing it was common for robbers to trick do-gooders with decoys like this man. He invested himself in aiding this stranger. His time, his effort, his attention during the night were all precious gifts. With unselfish grace, he spent his own travel funds to provide for the welfare of his newfound comrade. Two silver denarii equaled two days' wages—a substantial sum. Finally, he obligated himself to further expenses, whatever they might have been.

Today God may place in your path someone who needs compassion. Will you set aside your excuses and show love? The Good Samaritan is a model for us. In the name of Jesus, we must go and do likewise.

Dear Lord, the example of the Good Samaritan is a challenge to me. While helping others is a fine ideal, I often find it hard to live that way. Help me to have true compassion for the needy and, by your grace, to rescue the perishing.

INSIGHT

The Good Samaritan knew first-century first aid. He dressed the victim's wounds with oil, wine, and bandages. Wine, because of its alcohol content, would

Traveler beware! The rugged terrain of the Jericho Road in the Judean wilderness affords a would-be robber plenty of places to hide.

work like a disinfectant, killing germs. Oil served as an ointment. The bandages would prevent new bacteria from entering the wound. The Good Samaritan did all he could to provide immediate assistance and long-term care.

ENRICHMENT

The common inn of Jesus' day was a simple building consisting of several rooms adjacent to an open courtyard with a well at its center. The innkeeper supplied food and basic provisions for the travelers and their animals. While inns usually had a dubious reputation, they did provide water, relative safety, and shelter from the elements.

Today's Good Samaritan Inn is rebuilt on the site of ruins that are held by tradition as the location of the original inn. As you wander the grounds and sit by the well, contemplate the plight of the man in Jesus' story. The righteous and religious refused to help. It took the love of a stranger and a foreigner to rescue him.

While compassion always costs, reaching out to others is more convenient today than centuries ago. You will notice that the Good Samaritan Inn now takes VISA™.

JACOB'S WELL

BIBLE BACKGROUND: John 4:4–26

Tired Travelers

"Those who drink of the water that I will give them will never be thirsty. The water that I will give will become in them a spring of water gushing up to eternal life."

John 4:14 (NRSV)

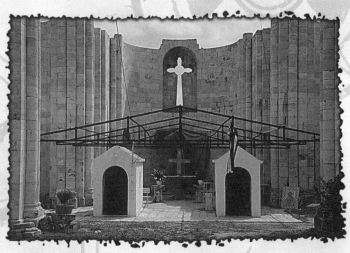

Jacob's Well, twenty feet beneath this uncompleted church, is considered the authentic site. The well still offers clear, cool water to its visitors.

As any tired traveler knows, there's nothing like a drink of clear, cool water to quench the thirst and refresh the soul. And so Jesus, hot and sweaty from a half day's journey, shuffled up to Jacob's Well. While His disciples bought lunch in the nearby village, He rested and waited for someone who could draw water to slake His thirst.

To the well came a woman who was also tired. She had carried her water jar to this place during the heat of the day. All her life she had borne the Jewish-imposed stigma common to all Samaritans—by race considered a half-breed, by religion, a fool. As a woman, she had felt

the constant disdain of men. Having known five hus-
bands and now living unmarried with a sixth man, her
sin burden was no doubt the heaviest of all. Tired in
body, soul, and spirit, she approached Jesus with obvious
defensiveness and anxiety.

But Jesus surprised her by requesting a drink. His attitude proved He was different from other Jewish men. Then
He offered her a gift—living water that would quench her
thirst forever. The water He gave would revive her with-
ering spirit and renew her dry and desperate life.

Not yet fully understanding but believing nonetheless, she accepted Jesus' gracious offer. As the living
water flooded her soul, it washed away her sin and
transformed her life.

As a road-weary traveler, Jesus provided a connection with which this life-weary woman could identify. At Jacob's ancient well, she met the Savior who
poured love into her dry and empty heart.

*Lord Jesus Christ, you are the only Source for living water.
You satisfy my soul and fulfill the spiritual longings of my heart.*

INSIGHT

Jacob's Well is one of the most authentic sites in all
Israel. The site accepted by all traditions is located today
in an unfinished Greek Orthodox church just east of Tel
Balatah, thought to be the location of ancient Shechem.
This spring-fed well is still deep, 75 feet (23 m), and is
known for its soft, drinkable water.

ENRICHMENT

Today the tired traveler reaches Jacob's Well by
descending more than a dozen steps to a crypt beneath
the floor of the church. Marble and tile overlay the
ancient limestone, and ornamental lamps hang from the
arched ceiling. Try to picture this place as it was in Jesus'
day—simple, rustic, and drenched in golden sunshine.

Point of Departure

But Jonah ran away from the LORD and headed for Tarshish. He went down to Joppa, where he found a ship bound for that port. After paying the fare, he went aboard and sailed for Tarshish to flee from the LORD.

Jonah 1:3

The Mediterranean port of Jaffa blushes in the setting sun.

Joppa is known today as Jaffa. Although its name has been altered, its significance remains. For many, this ancient harbor was the gateway to the glories of the Middle East. For Jonah, however, Joppa was the point of departure in his flight from God.

If you have ever received an assignment from God that you didn't like, then you know how Jonah felt when

God told him to preach to the people of Nineveh. These people were the enemies of Israel. They were notoriously nasty. They had been cruel to God's people. So Jonah refused to proclaim God's message of salvation for fear the Ninevites would repent and be spared the judgment he felt they deserved.

Jonah's rebellion was marked by three stages. First, he refused and ran. Joppa was his point of departure in his flight from God. "But Jonah ran away from the Lord and headed for Tarshish. He went down to Joppa, where he found a ship bound for that port" (1:3).

For a young adult, the point of departure may be a college town. Here the rebel discovers some worldly philosophy that will carry him away from God. Or the point of departure could be a new job in a different city. The change makes it difficult to find a new church, and the drift away from God begins.

When Jonah ran from God, he also relied on his own resources. Having found a ship bound for a faraway destination, he paid his own fare (1:3). Disobedience has a price tag that the rebel himself pays. No one else can pick up the tab.

Finally, Jonah was ruined and returned. He ended up doing what God requested, but his obedience came only after his ruin.

When we are faced with a choice to obey God or run, we encounter the same dilemma Jonah did. We must transform the potential point of departure into a port of discovery by obeying the Lord and relying on His grace.

Keep my heart soft and responsive, O God, so I may remain obedient to your will. Then each potential point of departure can be transformed into a port of discovery.

INSIGHT

The ancient harbor of Joppa may be the world's oldest active seaport. Although it is not used for significant commercial trade at present (the primary harbor being moved north), it remains a pleasant place for small sail boats and recreational craft. The archeologist's spade has turned up indications that this port may have been utilized four thousand years ago.

ENRICHMENT

Today a smiling bronze whale is beached on a concrete island in one of Jaffa's busy streets. Why is he smiling? Is he laughing at the silly tourists who have their picture taken with him? Or is he just happy to be rid of the rebel Jonah?

Strategy for Victory

The seventh time around, when the priests sounded the trumpet blast, Joshua commanded the people, "Shout! For the Lord has given you the city!"

Joshua 6:16

A bountiful freshwater spring helps keep the modern city of Jericho green year-round.

Doing right doesn't always *feel* right. Sometimes it feels foolish. It must have felt odd to march silently around a walled city for seven days and then erupt with a mighty shout. Yet this was how God told His people to go about conquering Jericho, the first stronghold of Canaan.

When we analyze this strategy for victory, we discover it had four elements.

The first was *obedience*. God gave Joshua the divine plan for conquest, and Joshua obediently relayed the plan to the people. Then the people chose whether or not to follow. With one million Jews crossing into the Promised Land, this plan had one million chances to break down. But it didn't. The Israelites followed obediently even though they didn't understand how it was going to work. Maybe they felt silly. Maybe they wondered what Jericho's inhabitants were thinking. But they were obedient. They did it.

Second, God's strategy for victory required *cooperation*. The various interest groups had to work together. The military went out first. Next came the priests, the religious block. Finally the general population followed. Note that there were two groups of leaders in front. While leaders often contend with each other, God's plan succeeds only as they cooperate. When leaders lead with unity, the people follow.

Third, victory required *persistence*. God had His people literally going in circles, yet they kept on. They repeated the same procedure six days in a row. They went through the same routine seven more times on the seventh day. By faithfully sticking to the program, they proved their persistence to God and to themselves.

Fourth, God's strategy required *faith*. There was no logical reason to expect the seventh march on the seventh day to be more effective than the previous twelve times around. Yet at that point, Joshua issued the command to shout. That shout took faith. It required confidence in God and in Joshua, their leader. Plus it demonstrated trust in a spiritual strategy that, frankly, made no military sense.

This same strategy can enable us to triumph over barriers that stand in our way: obedience to God even when it feels wrong; cooperation with our leaders and others; persistence even when we feel like quitting; and faith that claims the victory even before it is visible.

You, O God, are a mighty warrior who knows how to give victory to His people. And since your strategy always requires something of me, I commit myself to obedience, cooperation, persistence, and faith. Together we will achieve success.

INSIGHT

Oddly enough for the Bible student, what we want to see is not here. Although archeologists have declared differing opinions throughout the years, it is now generally accepted that the walls that tumbled under Joshua's leadership no longer exist. Some guides and literature still point to certain sun-dried brick walls as being those of Joshua's day. However, Kathleen Kenyon's excavations (1952–58) identify those same walls as coming from the Early Bronze Age—much older than the Jericho of Joshua's day.

Actually, it makes sense that the walls Joshua demolished, burned, and left scattered would no longer exist. Broken pieces of earthen and stone wall left exposed to winter rains for hundreds of years could not be expected to last in any recognizable form. The curse that Joshua pronounced over Jericho (6:26) held true. No one rebuilt this city until Hiel of Bethel attempted it five hundred years later (1 Kings 16:34). By then the remnants of Joshua's Jericho had disappeared.

ENRICHMENT

Nowhere in Israel does history display more depth than at Tel es-Sultan, the site of ancient Jericho. Here you will find the ruins of a wall, moat, and round tower that archeologists date to the seventh millennium B.C. Let your eyes rest on these ancient ruins of mud and stone, and try to grasp the antiquity of something nine thousand years old! Now you know why Jericho is often titled "the oldest city in the world."

Looking for Love

Jesus said to him, "Today salvation has come to this house, because this man, too, is a son of Abraham. For the Son of Man came to seek and to save what was lost."

Luke 19:9–10

Although it is certainly not two thousand years old, this tree in modern-day Jericho is sometimes referred to as "Zacchaeus' sycamore."

Zacchaeus knew it long before the Beatles sang it: "Money can't buy me love." While Zacchaeus was one of Jericho's richest men, he was at the same time one of its least-loved citizens.

Jericho flourished as a key commercial center in the first century. Known as the "City of Palms," it was a tropical paradise where the rich and famous loved to live. Its balmy climate and prolific spring produced world-famous balsam and beautiful roses. Major trade routes crisscrossed at Jericho and brought prosperity to its doorstep. Here Zacchaeus carried on a lucrative tax business for the Romans. He probably feathered his own nest in the process.

Considered a traitor by his countrymen and a thief by all, Zacchaeus had climbed to the highest position—a "chief tax collector." But he was despised by his neighbors, an outcast of society. Loneliness haunted him and love was nowhere to be found.

But Zacchaeus was desperately looking for love. Having heard that Jesus, "a friend of tax collectors and sinners," was coming to town, he determined to see Him.

Short, round, and close to the ground, Zacchaeus could not see over the crowds, so he adopted an unusual strategy. He ran down the road and scrambled up into a tree. Such an odd sight surely made folks snicker. But Zacchaeus didn't care what people thought. They already despised him. He had nothing to lose and everything to gain.

When Jesus saw Zacchaeus perched in the sycamore-fig branches, He said, "Today I must come to your house." And Zacchaeus knew he had heard the words he longed for. Here was someone who would accept him. Finally someone who would break bread with him. At last he had found love.

Lord, I am like Zacchaeus—a sinner looking for love. In my search for acceptance, sometimes I resort to strange and desperate ways. Help me to rest in the assurance of your love.

INSIGHT

Three Jerichos draw the attention of tourists today. Tel es-Sultan is the site of ancient Jericho, the city of Joshua's conquest. To the south of the tel, lie the ruins of the New Testament city where Jesus met Zacchaeus. Present-day Jericho is a Palestinian-controlled city of more than one hundred thousand inhabitants.

ENRICHMENT

While in Jericho you may want to shop at the outlet store for Hebron glass. Since few tourists will venture to Hebron itself, this is a good opportunity to see and purchase a sample of the beautiful blown glassware.

A Mighty Fortress

The Lord is my rock, my fortress and my deliverer; my God is my rock, in whom I take refuge.

2 Samuel 22:2–3

For thousands of years Masada has offered a rocky refuge in the Judean wilderness west of the Dead Sea. This view from the west shows the Dead Sea and the country of Jordan in the background.

Masada is an awesome natural fortress. Rising nearly 1000 feet (300 m) high, this massive mesa of rugged rock stands in the Dead Sea wilderness as a symbol of strength and security. Its very name means mountain fortress.

For thousands of years it has served as a place to run and hide. Kings, zealots, and fugitives have looked to it for protection in times of trouble. Herod the Great recognized the natural advantages of this high hideaway and built a palace and fort there. Thirty years later, Masada became the last stronghold for zealots and patriots fleeing Roman oppression.

Repeatedly the Bible uses the image of a rock to speak of the strength, rest, and protection that God provides His children. Moses' first reference in Deuteronomy 32:4 calls on His people to praise the greatness of God for "He is the Rock." And Paul uses the same metaphor to refer to Christ declaring Him the spiritual rock (1 Corinthians 10:4).

In a land where deforestation and erosion have stripped the land and exposed its naked bones, the rock is a ready and easily recognized metaphor. For those familiar with a different geography the symbolism is more difficult. Nonetheless, the rock has become a prevalent symbol in Christian church liturgy. Augustus M. Toplady's beloved "Rock of Ages" remains a favorite of the generations.

When our enemy the devil pursues us, God is the Rock to which we can run. Satan prowls around seeking spiritual prey, but the hunted can flee to the Rock and find protection. There is a way of escape and a haven of safety in our God.

When our integrity is attacked, our Rock provides a place that is steadfast and sure. No human being can know with certainty the motive of another's heart. Yet God searches the heart and examines the mind, to give to all according to their ways (Jeremiah 17:10). He knows our intent and rewards our integrity though no one else may understand.

When gossips hiss and strike at our heels, the only safe ground is to retreat to the Rock. There we find peace and rest knowing that God is the God of truth and our reputation is in His almighty hands.

Where can we find protection from the evil one, inner security, and personal peace? Only in God who is greater than all our foes. When hounded by hostile forces, we must run to the Rock.

You, O God, are a mighty fortress. When I run to you, I am secure from all my foes.

These round-cut stones were probably used by Masada's defenders to bowl would-be attackers off the cliff face.

INSIGHT

In A.D. 73 the last Jewish patriots to occupy Masada gave up their lives rather than surrender their freedom. The trusted Jewish historian, Josephus, tells how the 960 men, women, and children living on Masada met their deaths. Archeologists have unearthed bits and pieces which seem to confirm the record.

When it appeared inevitable that the Romans would capture Masada, Eleazar Ben Yai'r delivered a passionate appeal to his followers. He described the horror awaiting the defenders if they became Roman prisoners. He begged them to choose mass suicide rather than surrender.

Each man slew his own family and burned their possessions. Then by lot, ten men were chosen to kill all the heads of households. When they had done their deed, they regathered. Each man's name was scrawled on a fragment of pottery. One lot was chosen. That man slew his companions. And finally, Josephus says, "he drove his sword through his own body."

The spirit of freedom still swirls around Masada's crest. It inspires the Israelis in their struggles. It touches every visitor. The memory of Masada lives on.

ENRICHMENT

Have your picture taken beside the rough-hewn stone "cannonballs" which are piled together on Masada's plateau. Use it as a reminder. No earthly or spiritual weapon can shake your security in the Lord. Almighty God is your refuge and strength.

Alone With Temptation

[Jesus was] tempted in every way, just as we are—yet was without sin. Let us then approach the throne of grace with confidence, so that we may receive mercy and find grace to help us in our time of need.

Hebrews 4:15-16

The Mount of Temptation (viewed from the west) is riddled with caves, making it a haven for wild animals (Mark 1:13).

Do you ever wonder where the gospel writers got their facts about the temptation of Christ? They weren't present. Our Lord was all alone in a desolate place for forty days. It must be that Jesus Himself supplied them with the information. He revealed His experience to them, so that they could tell us, and we could be helped by knowing what He endured.

While this portion of Scripture is usually referred to as "The Temptation of Jesus," it really is a misleading title. There was not one temptation, but three. And certainly this was not the only time Jesus was tempted. As Luke indicated (4:13), the devil attacked Jesus on other occasions as well. It is fair to say Jesus was tempted His entire life. But this account presents us with three practical insights.

The first insight deals with *timing*. Some of life's toughest temptations come on the heels of our highest spiritual moments. This time of terrible temptation followed immediately after Jesus' baptism and personal affirmation from the Father. He was boosted by His Father, then blasted by His adversary. Our spiritual victories do not end with a laurel wreath so often as they signal the beginning of the next battle.

The second insight reveals Jesus' temptation as *typical*. The devil will tempt us in every area where he thinks we are vulnerable. The three temptations of Jesus often are interpreted as indicating three areas in which we may be tempted. Some see them as temptations in the physical, spiritual, and emotional realms. Others classify them as John does—the lust of the flesh, the lust of the eyes, and the pride of life (1 John 2:16). Whatever the classification, we know that the devil will shoot at every chink in our armor.

The third insight presents Jesus' *tactic*. We can find victory over temptation when we use God's Word as a sword of Truth. Jesus quoted Scripture in His defense against the devil, and so can we. In every instance it worked. When Jesus quoted the Bible, the devil had no reply. We, too, can strengthen our defenses against temptation by memorizing and utilizing the power of God's word.

Jesus revealed this episode of His life to His followers so that they could benefit from His example. He also did it so that we would know we are not alone when we face temptations. He was alone; we are not. He is with us to help us and strengthen us. We can be victorious just as He was.

Here I come, Lord. I approach your throne of grace to receive the help you have promised. Because you were tempted in every way that I am, you know what I need.

INSIGHT

Since scholars debate the locale of Jesus' baptism, it follows that they also debate the place of His temptation. If Jesus' baptism was in the Jericho area, as many claim, then where is the "very high mountain" that Matthew speaks of (4:8)? Tradition points to Mount Quarantania. Its name is derived from the same word from which we get our English word *quarantine*. Originally, it meant a period of isolation lasting forty days.

The Greek Orthodox Church has built a monastery on this mountain. It is difficult to spot because it hangs on the face of the cliff and blends in so well. Binoculars make it easier, but you can see it with the naked eye. Look about halfway down from the peak and a little to the left.

Most tours will not have time to visit the monastery, but those who do will be rewarded with an impressive view. All of Jericho, known as the "City of Palms," and the mountains of Moab, including Mount Nebo, capture the attention as you gaze eastward.

ENRICHMENT

Mark's brief account of Jesus' temptation includes an interesting fact. He alone reports that during Jesus' forty days in the desert, "He was with the wild animals" (1:13). Mark stresses the physical danger Jesus faced while alone in such an untamed environment.

This raises some intriguing questions. Where did Jesus sleep? What shelter did He have from the blazing sun and the blistering heat? How did He keep wild animals at bay? A likely solution to this puzzle may be that He stayed in a cave.

When you visit Jericho, your guide will point out the traditional Mount of Temptation, west of the city. As you scan this barren brown bluff, note how many caves are carved in its face. Could Jesus have taken shelter in one of these?

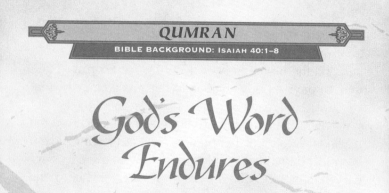

God's Word Endures

The grass withers and the flowers fall, but the word of our God stands forever.

Isaiah 40:8

When Cave IV surrendered its treasures into the hands of eager archeologists, it yielded more than 4000 manuscripts and about 1000 additional fragments!

When the tiny religious community of Qumran fled before the Roman invasion of A.D. 68, they left behind their most precious possessions sealed in earthenware jars and hidden in caves. Although they did not leave gold or precious jewels, what they abandoned have been called "the greatest historical treasures of the world." These are the Dead Sea Scrolls, and in three ways they strengthen our confidence in the reliability of God's Word.

First, they confirm the accuracy of our modern Bible versions. These two-thousand-year-old Scripture scrolls are essentially identical to the texts we use today. Thus, they prove our Bible is an accurate and reliable transmission of what the Old Testament writers first penned. No one has tampered with the texts. From the account of creation to the predictions of Christ's future kingdom, the Bible remains unchanged.

Second, they demonstrate the scribes' meticulous care in copying the manuscripts. The Dead Sea Scrolls are word-for-word identical with the texts modern translators use. The only deviations after two millennia are a few slips of the pen and variations in spelling. As Jesus declared, "I tell you the truth, until heaven and earth disappear, not the smallest letter, not the least stroke of a pen, will by any means disappear from the Law until everything is accomplished" (Matthew 5:18).

Third, the Dead Sea Scrolls prove the trustworthiness of God's promises. If God said it, we can count on it. Nothing changes the commitments and covenants of God. As the prophet Isaiah emphasized: "The grass withers and the flowers fall, but the word of our God stands forever" (40:8).

For two thousand years this very verse lay rolled up and wrapped in linen, stuffed in a clay jar, and sealed. Its existence awaited rediscovery. But its truth has been acknowledged by generations: God's Word endures.

Eternal God, I am grateful for your written Word, the Holy Bible. Thank you for preserving it down through the ages so I can rely upon it as the Word of Truth today.

The Dead Sea Scrolls are a collection of some forty thousand fragments and a number of complete manuscripts that comprise the whole or partial text of some five hundred books. Included in this cache are portions of every Old Testament book except Esther and two copies of the entire book of Isaiah.

In 1947 a Bedouin shepherd boy went looking for a lost goat in these cave-riddled hills. Throwing a stone

A group of Christians gather in the Scriptorium to hear their guide's explanation of how this room may have been the place where the holy Scriptures were copied by hand.

into the mouth of a cave, he heard a curious "clink." Upon investigation, he found several large terra-cotta jars on the floor of the cave, each containing a leather scroll carefully wrapped in linen cloth.

Ironically, the first person he offered to sell them to refused, reckoning them unworthy of the 20-pound asking price. After weeks of bargaining, they were sold to interested parties in Jerusalem. Later, just four of these ancient manuscripts were resold to the Israeli government for $250,000!

The tower platform offers an excellent place from which to view the ruins of Qumran. As you look south, your gaze falls on the 43 by 13 foot (13 by 4 m) room where three ink wells were found. Many call it the scriptorium, believing it to be the place where the Holy Scriptures and other manuscripts were copied.

Beyond the remains of the settlement to the east, lie the marl cliffs where more than forty caves have been examined by archeologists. Eleven of these have yielded manuscript material. Ask your guide to point out Cave IV where the first, and perhaps the most momentous, discoveries were made.

Seven original scrolls found in Cave IV are now displayed in The Shrine of the Book. This striking and symbolic museum is well worth a visit when you are in Jerusalem.

Life's Memorial Markers

So Rachel died and was buried on the way to Ephrath (that is, Bethlehem). Over her tomb Jacob set up a pillar, and to this day that pillar marks Rachel's tomb.

Genesis 35:19–20

Rachel's true final resting place is somewhere in the fertile hills around Bethlehem.

The road of life needs markers. Something in human nature demands that we keep track of significant events with celebrations, keepsakes, and tangible memorials. Young sweethearts may carve their initials in a tree and encircle them with a heart. Years later one erects a granite headstone over the grave of the other.

Since the dawn of human history, people have been raising monuments at significant points in their lives.

Jacob was particularly fond of erecting "pillars" or memorial stones. When God blessed him at Bethel and promised to bring him safely back to his homeland, Jacob set up a pillar (Genesis 28:18). He marked the covenant with his brother-in-law Laban in the same way (Genesis 31:45). And upon his safe return to Bethel, Jacob set up another stone pillar as a memorial to God's faithfulness (Genesis 35:14).

As the patriarch and his family caravanned south toward Bethlehem, Jacob's favorite wife, Rachel, went into labor with their second son. Unfortunately, she died in childbirth, and Jacob marked her grave with yet another memorial pillar.

For Jacob these stones were not only markers for significant events, but they also served as worship aids. They were visible reminders of God's protection, provision, faithfulness, and sovereignty. As such, the stones were transformed into literal and symbolic altars.

Today Christians have a memorial that focuses our worship on God's provision of spiritual salvation. In the Lord's Supper we remember the death, burial, and resurrection of our Lord Jesus Christ. This living memorial is lifted up as a tangible reminder of the cross, which marks life's most significant turning point.

Lord, if the death of a loved one deserves a marker to make it more memorable, how much more the death of our Savior? In every observance of communion. let me raise my heart in worship and praise.

INSIGHT

Scholars debate the location of Rachel's Tomb. Certainly the present structure is not Jacob's monument, for the small, domed building just north of Bethlehem dates from the eighteenth and nineteenth centuries. But tradition, the Talmud, and the opinions of Origen, Eusebius, Jerome, and Josephus all weigh in on the side of this site's authenticity.

Wherever Rachel's bones actually rest, one thing is for sure: she was the only matriarch not buried in Hebron. While Sarah, Rebekah, and even Leah were laid to rest in the Cave of Machpelah, Rachel was not.

ENRICHMENT

Rachel's Tomb is often a drive-by site for Christians on a Holy Land tour. Tourists rushing to see Jesus' birthplace often can't stop long enough for even a quick click of the camera. Yet this place is holy to Jews and Muslims alike, and it is especially revered by women, who, like Rachel, struggle with infertility. Inside you might hear the tearful prayer of a desperate woman longing for a child. And you may also observe someone winding a red thread seven times around Rachel's tomb marker. Pieces of this hallowed thread are used as charms and cure-alls for those who believe.

Beware Greener Pastures

Lot looked up and saw that the whole plain of the Jordan was well watered . . . . So Lot chose for himself the whole plain of the Jordan and set out toward the east.

Genesis 13:10–11

Located west of the southern tip of the Dead Sea, Mount Sodom may indicate the general vicinity of the biblical city known by the same name.

The quest for greener pastures often leads downhill. Lot's pursuit of worldly success cost him his wealth, his wife, and nearly his life. What he thought was his path to prosperity turned out to be the road to ruin.

By the blessing of God, both Abram and his nephew Lot had grown extremely wealthy. The day came when the land could no longer support the large flocks of them both. So Abram suggested they part company in order to stay friends. To this, Lot readily agreed, but he stumbled on the way to independence.

His first misstep came when he chose for himself, without concern for the welfare of others. Given the opportunity to select any pasture he wanted, Lot grabbed the prime real estate and left his uncle with the less desirable land. The culture of the Middle East would dictate that, as the younger person, he should have deferred to his uncle's best interests. But selfishness won out over respect for his elder relative.

Lot stumbled again when he surveyed the green grass of the valley and failed to look any deeper. He concluded greener pastures meant a better life, but he did not weigh the impact the inhabitants of the valley could have on his household. Had he dug beneath the surface, he might have discovered that the soil that made for good grazing was unsuitable for growing a godly family.

Lot's most critical error was to value worldly wealth more than spiritual health. When he pitched his tents near Sodom, he moved closer to a moral cesspool. Already "the men of Sodom were wicked and were sinning greatly against the Lord" (13:13). Perhaps he thought he was strong enough to withstand its downward draw, but as Genesis later records, Lot's greed for greener pastures compromised the spiritual vitality of his whole family.

Many times temptations are keener where the grass is greener. One must be careful to scrutinize the situation in light of its potential impact on spiritual life. As Matthew Henry noted, ". . . that is best for us which is best for our souls."

You, O Lord, are the Good Shepherd who makes me lie down in green pastures. Make me content with your provision so that I will not wander from your side, seeking what looks greener.

INSIGHT

Sodom and Gomorrah have become infamous for their sin. In fact, throughout the Old and New Testaments alike, their names have become synonymous with immorality and are symbols for the judgment of God. Jesus Himself uses their wickedness as a standard for judgment (Matthew 10:15).

After their fire-and-brimstone devastation (Genesis 19), Sodom and Gomorrah are never again mentioned as inhabited cities. Therefore, no one can be certain of their location. Most Bible scholars believe that they were situated somewhere near the southern end of the Dead Sea. Many speculate that their ruins lie beneath the salty shallows south of the Lisan Peninsula.

ENRICHMENT

The Bible records that, because Lot's wife disregarded the angel's warning and looked back toward Sodom, she became a pillar of salt (Genesis 19:26). On the slopes of Mount Sodom, west of the Dead Sea, stands a formation some have dubbed "Lot's Wife." A picture of such a pillar could serve as a warning today for contemporary Christians who long for greener pastures. Without the blessing of God, all appealing pastures turn brown and return to dust.

Giant-Size Pride

Pride goes before destruction, a haughty spirit before a fall.
Proverbs 16:18

The white limestone hills along the Valley of Elah provided excellent vantage points for opposing armies to gather and taunt each other before battle.

Goliath was a giant man and a great warrior, but he perished because of his pride.

More than nine feet (3 m) tall, he towered over his shepherd-boy opponent. He was a professional warrior, a "champion," who had trained for personal combat since his youth.

Although the Philistines occupied a narrow strip of land along the Mediterranean Sea in the southwestern part of Israel, their ancestry was European. Therefore, Goliath's armor was most likely of Aegean design.

Goliath entered battle well prepared. With coat of mail, leg armor, and helmet all of bronze, his vital organs were protected. His personal shield-bearer provided extra defense. He carried a sword, a javelin, and an iron-tipped spear. His helmet likely had a visor like those worn by sword-and-spear-fighters of the day. This visor was designed to deflect a blow to the head and protect the fighter's brow.

What a contrast was David. Having rejected Saul's armor, he wore only shepherd's garb. No armor, no helmet, no shield— his only weapon was a simple sling and five smooth stones.

When the great and mighty Goliath saw his humble opponent, pride filled his heart. In contempt he cursed David. It takes little imagination to see Goliath rear back his head and laugh.

At that moment of pride, Goliath was most vulnerable. When his head went back and his nose went up, he exposed his forehead as a target for David's sling. Rushing forward, sling in motion, David let fly the fatal blow, and Goliath came toppling down.

Standing in the Valley of Elah today, one can almost hear Goliath's proud taunts bounce off the rocky banks. His self-confidence arrogance still echoes as a warning to all. A nose in the air is a target for defeat.

Lord, keep me from foolish pride. Remind me that confidence in the flesh is an invitation to disaster.

INSIGHT

Valley of Elah means "Valley of Terebinth," so named because of the many terebinth trees in the vicinity. This valley is generally identified today as Wadi es-Sant, a gully located 11 miles (17.6 km) southwest of Jerusalem. Its high banks are relatively close to each other, so you can picture the opposing armies shouting back and forth to each other.

This spot is a natural battlefield for the Philistines and the Israelites because of its location between their respective territories. Its banks offer ideal positions for each army to occupy and defend. The location of so many battles, it is sometimes referred to as the "Valley of Blood."

ENRICHMENT

The Valley of Elah is dry most of the year. Only during the rainy season will you find an actual stream flowing through this steep-banked ravine. Nonetheless, the creek bed is filled with stones just like David collected to use against Goliath. Choose five smooth stones to take home. As you feel the stones in your pocket, remind yourself of the spiritual dynamics of this battle. David achieved victory over Goliath because he was a humble soldier operating in the name of the Lord.

By the way, if you wonder whether it is legal to take rocks from the Holy Land, check with your guide. There are so many rocks in Israel, the government allows tourists to carry away up to eighty pounds (36 kg) per person!

Galilee

Tragedy of Unfaithfulness

Saul died because he was unfaithful to the Lord; he did not keep the word of the Lord. . . . So the Lord put him to death and turned the kingdom over to David son of Jesse.

1 Chronicles 10:13–14

Extensive Roman-era ruins cover acres at the base of tel Beth Shan.

A leader's unfaithfulness to God often results in a shameful demise. The tragic circumstances of King Saul's death depict the depths to which the mighty may fall when they wander from the will of God.

Chosen by God to be the first king over the nation of Israel, Saul started with great promise. He was blessed with natural strength, administrative skill, and military prowess. Yet he never entirely submitted his temperament and talents to God's direction. Thus, the end of his life was marked, not by honor, but by five degrees of disgrace.

The first degree was *personal*. While certain cultures view suicide in time of adversity as noble, God's people regard it as always dishonorable and wrong. When Saul decided to die by his own hand, he chose the lowest way out.

The drama of his last day was also *familial*. When Saul died, he took his whole house with him. The royal father and three sons, including the popular and noble Jonathan, were killed on the same battlefield. While the death of the king was tragic, the simultaneous loss of his heirs was disastrous.

Saul's death meant *national* calamity, too. All his life Saul had defended Israel from enemy assault. His death now signaled a Philistine advance unequaled in history and unparalleled in scope.

But perhaps the greatest shame in Saul's death was *spiritual*. The end of his life was exploited as an opportunity for praise of pagan gods. The Scriptures tell us that his head was hung in Dagon's temple as a trophy of victory (1 Chronicles 10:10), and his armor was placed as a votive offering in the temple of the Ashtoreths.

The final degree of disgrace caused by Saul's death was *international*. When the Philistines pinned his headless corpse to the wall of Beth Shan, they made a strategic choice. Situated at the junction of the Jezreel and Jordan Valleys, Beth Shan controlled the crossroads of major highways. With Galilee and Damascus to the north, the Mediterranean to the west, and Jerusalem to the south, travelers from many nations passed through this prominent city. Here in this public place, Saul's fallen form was a silent witness to the triumph of the pagan powers. While thousands of residents whispered about it, tens of thousands of travelers trumpeted the news in every direction.

These five degrees of disgrace were the solemn epitaph of one who fulfilled the worst in his death because he failed to live up to the best in his life.

Almighty God, you have power over princes and paupers. I want to be faithful to your Word, so that in death, as in life, I may influence others to draw closer to you.

INSIGHT

Strangely enough, while Beth Shan is mentioned frequently in the Bible, it played a very small role in Israel's history. Although allotted to the tribe of Manasseh (Joshua 17:11), it was not conquered until David's day. Solomon made it the capital of one of his northern administrative districts (1 Kings 4:12), but under Rehoboam it fell again into heathen hands (1 Kings 14:25).

Archeologists delight to uncover such beautiful specimens as this column and capital at Beth Shan.

Nonetheless, its ruins are noteworthy. The ancient theater is the largest in all Israel with an estimated capacity of seven thousand. Its first tier is completely preserved and offers the visitor a spectacular example of Roman architecture.

Beth Shan (or Bet She'an) is the site of Israel's most extensive archeological excavation and restoration project. While most of the exposed ruins date to Roman times, evidence of occupation has been discovered as early as the fifth millennium B.C. In fact, about twenty levels of civilization have been uncovered.

You can grasp the scope of this ancient city best if you take the time to walk all the way around it. And be sure to climb the tel itself. Its present top layer goes back to Joshua's day. From there you can see Mount Gilboa, where King Saul committed suicide rather than be captured by the Philistines. And you can get an idea of the strategic location this ancient city enjoyed.

Take a private moment in some quiet spot to reflect upon the greatness of the glory that is now gone. Here thousands have lived, died, and passed into eternity without hope. Here a man with so much potential died with so little honor. What will you learn from his example?

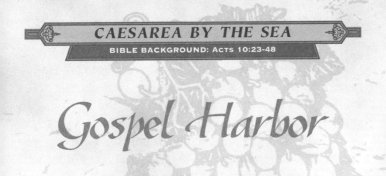

Gospel Harbor

The human mind may devise many plans, but it is the purpose of the Lord that will be established.

Proverbs 19:21 (NRSV)

Caesarea's extensive ruins stretch along the eastern edge of the Mediterranean Sea.

Kings rule, but God overrules. And such was the case with Herod.

As the Rome-appointed ruler of the Jews, Herod needed to make it easy for the Roman legions to access their occupied territory. To accomplish this, he had two options: Take over Haifa, Israel's only natural harbor, or create a new port somewhere else along the Mediterranean coast.

If he chose to station Roman soldiers in Haifa where strong Jewish factions were well-established, he risked constant conflict between the oppressed and their oppressors. Whereas, if he could keep the Jews and Romans physically separate, perhaps he could also keep their ideas separate. Less contact would hopefully result in fewer problems.

Thus, Herod chose a much more expensive but potentially more peaceful solution—create an entirely new port city. Caesarea was that city. Herod took an insignificant town and in twelve years transformed it into a municipality so magnificent it was dubbed "Little Rome." Its man-made harbor was a feat of engineering so fantastic that modern scholars still marvel. When Herod dedicated this city to Caesar, he also made it the capital of Roman power for all Judea.

Ironically, with the building of Caesarea, Herod created a port of entry for the gospel. Where Herod wanted separation, God willed salvation. God's divine intention has always been to spread the gospel of Jesus to every nation. As a strategic step in that process, God arranged an encounter between a Roman seeker and a Jewish Christian preacher. Caesarea was the site of that meeting.

When the apostle Peter explained the way of salvation to Cornelius, he readily received it. There in Caesarea, his Roman duty-station, Cornelius became the first recorded Gentile convert to Christianity.

Cornelius was uniquely prepared by God for a key role in spreading the gospel. As a Gentile, he provided a human link for a Savior with Jewish heritage to reach an entirely different segment of humanity. As a Roman centurion in charge of a hundred soldiers, his testimony would be heard and respected wherever he went. As a man of great influence, he led his relatives and close friends to respond immediately to Peter's message of good news. Following Cornelius' conversion, a Christian church was established in Caesarea.

With more than a dozen New Testament references to Caesarea, we know it played a prominent role in Christianity's early days. Philip the evangelist lived and witnessed there. The apostle Paul reasoned with Felix, Festus, and Agrippa during his two-year imprisonment there. Indeed, Caesarea was Paul's launching point for many of his missionary journeys.

Although Herod planned to keep the Jews and the Romans separate, God overruled. The gospel must not be isolated. The divine plan has always been for those who know the truth to mingle, share, and witness.

The same is true today. The walls of communism once raised against the gospel in Eastern Europe and the former U.S.S.R. have crumbled. Now freedom in Christ is openly proclaimed and thousands are turning to Jesus. Even in China, the world's largest bastion of communism, God is proving that He is sovereign. Conservative estimates count 20 to 30 million Christian believers in China today, and more are turning to the Savior daily.

Sometimes in our private worlds we encounter human hindrances to the gospel. Office politics restrain the individual who tries to take a stand for Christ. School regulations limit the ways a student may witness. Secular college professors stack the deck against young scholars who try to stand for truth in the classroom. These contemporary barriers are erected in hopes of containing the good news of Jesus Christ. For a while it may appear to work, but in the long run, it cannot. God is sovereign and He is able to remove any barrier and create a harbor for the gospel.

INSIGHT

Bible skeptics once doubted Luke's accuracy as a historian. For example, since Pilate's name could not be found in records other than the Bible (Luke 3:1), they reasoned he did not exist. However, in 1961 a large fragment of a dedication slab was unearthed in Caesarea. Its Latin inscription read, in part, "[Pon]tius Pilatus . . . Military Procurator." Today's visitor can read this inscription and know that the Bible is historically trustworthy.

ENRICHMENT

Thousands of pottery pieces are scattered on Caesarea's shores. Although they are worthless archeologically, they make valuable souvenirs for the treasure hunter who has spent a life's savings to get here. They are remnants of a city where Rome once ruled, but God overruled.

One True God

Simon Peter answered, "You are the Christ, the Son of the living God."
Matthew 16:16

This stream at Caesarea Philippi used to spill from the mouth of the cave seen here on the left. To the right, several niches remain that used to display Pan's image.

Today diversity is almost deified. Our pluralistic society demands more than mere tolerance of others' right to worship as they please. It requires acceptance of conflicting beliefs as equally true. This is nothing new, however. Caesarea Philippi has been a home for such pluralism for ages.

In Canaanite times this verdant park was a focus of Baal worship. In the fourth century B.C., the conquering Greeks established here a shrine to Pan who, like Baal, was a god of fertility. In 20 B.C. Herod the Great erected a white marble temple for worship of the Roman emperor Augustus Caesar. While worship of Pan continued, emperor worship was added.

To this pluralistic place known for various pagan religions came Jesus with His disciples. Certainly this beautiful spot afforded them a cool and pleasant setting for much-needed rest. Additionally it provided a perfect setting for Jesus to test His disciples' spiritual understanding. "Are there many gods or one? Who do people say the Son of Man is? Who do you say I am?" He asked.

Simon Peter's response was quick, clear, and exclusive: "You are the Christ, the Son of the living God." His answer was not a poll of public opinion. Nor was it a supplement to the surrounding pantheon. This was a revelation of God.

In our whirlpool of pluralistic equality this is what we need—a fresh revelation of the uniqueness of our Lord. He is not simply another god to be added to a personal list of acceptable deities. He is the "only begotten" or "one and only" Son of God as John recorded in his gospel (John 3:16).

Jesus' claims are exclusive. He stated plainly, "I am the way and the truth and the life. No one comes to the Father except through me" (John 14:6). He will tolerate no rivals. When He asserted Himself as the only way to God, He pushed aside all other possible candidates.

Nevertheless we hear many objections to Jesus as the only way. "That may be true for you, but I believe in a different truth." Or, "My god isn't like that." Or, "I've discovered that I am god." Such remarks are essentially rejections of Jesus as the one, true God. In opposition to such popular pluralism, the faithful Christian must stand with Peter and the other disciples in witness to Jesus as the Christ, the Son of the living God.

Lord Jesus Christ, in a society which wants to make all religions equal, I take my stand. You are the one true God. I bow my knee to no other.

INSIGHT

Caesarea Philippi has many secrets still hidden beneath her green mantle. Much of the area remains unexcavated. For example, the exact location of the Roman temple Herod built is not known.

However, she has revealed some of her ancient treasures. A cache of coins was discovered which show Pan in various poses. On one he leans against a tree and plays a flute. On another he appears in the mouth of the cavern. On a third, his panpipe is pictured. Other coins show the Roman temple and various figures.

ENRICHMENT

The niches where once Pan's statue stood are now fenced off. The cave from which this easternmost source of the Jordan once gushed is likewise off limits. But with binoculars or a telephoto lens, you can still go exploring. Carefully examine the cliff face. How many niches do you see?

Gather with your group around one of the broken columns or mossy stones. These scattered ruins are a silent testimony to a pagan god once worshiped at this site. With a chorus of "He Is Lord," you, like Peter, can affirm the supremacy of Jesus Christ.

God Is Good

"Everyone brings out the choice wine first and then the cheaper wine after the guests have had too much to drink; but you have saved the best till now."

John 2:10

This stone jar at the church of Cana symbolizes Jesus' miracle of turning water into wine.

"God is great, God is good," begins the preschooler's prayer. In those deceptively simple words is a message of profound truth for every believer, whether child or adult. Jesus' first miracle, performed at a wedding in Cana of Galilee, demonstrated both the greatness and the goodness of Jesus our God.

Jesus displayed His greatness as He proved His power over creation. He changed water into wine. Only He could take what was common and ordinary and transform it into something unique and distinctive. When the natural supply for the fruit of the vine gave out, the supernatural Source stepped in.

Jesus showed His goodness by the quantity and the quality of the wine He provided. Note what He did. The six water jars nearby could have held a total of 120–180 gallons (450–680 l). Those jars, filled to the brim, provided enough wine to gladden scores of people for many days! Jesus did not give a bare minimum. He gave in abundance.

When the master of the banquet tasted that unique vintage, he judged it the best that had been served. He complimented the bridegroom on the superior quality of that wine. Jesus gave such quality that no one could dispute its value.

This first miracle was a sign for all who had eyes to see. His grace was proved by the quantity and the quality of His gift. It was abundant. It was superior. It was free.

Jesus revealed His divine glory in this first miracle. By it He proved that God truly is great, and God surely is good.

Lord Jesus Christ, you are God. Your miracles prove your divinity, and they display your goodness and grace. I rejoice to know and worship you.

==========< INSIGHT >==========

As with so many religious sites in the Holy Land, the exact location of Cana is disputed. Of the two primary contenders, Kafr Cana is the most popular with tourists. Its churches, art, and artifacts provide something to visit, photograph, and appreciate. It is conveniently located 5 miles (8 km) northeast of Nazareth on the road to Tiberias. Tradition since ancient and medieval times has named this locale as the site of Jesus' first miracle. The church there even claims to have several stone jars used in the first miracle. It is conveniently located along the road between Nazareth and Tiberias. Most people are satisfied if their guide says, "This is Cana of Galilee, where Jesus performed His first miracle."

However, another location is favored today by many scholars as more likely the site of the biblical Cana. Khirbet Kana is about 10 miles (16 km) north of Nazareth and overlooks the Battof Valley that once was filled with reeds. Since *cana* in Hebrew means "reeds," this location seems a logical choice. Atop the hill an unexcavated ruin has yielded coins and pottery pieces that also point to this location as authentic.

Cana, like so many other religious sites in the Holy Land, leaves the Christian pilgrim with the challenge to worship the Person and not the place.

ENRICHMENT

If you are traveling through the Holy Land with your spouse, this is a meaningful place to renew your wedding vows. Invite others in your group to do the same. Since Jesus blessed the wedding at Cana with His presence and miraculous gift, what better place than this to ask Him to bless your marriage as well?

Bread of Heaven

I am the living bread that came down from heaven. Whoever eats of this bread will live forever. . . .

John 6:51 (NRSV)

The ancient synagogue at Capernaum maintains a certain splendor despite sixteen centuries of exposure to the sea air.

There is no such thing as a free lunch. We may want something for nothing, but in reality there is always a cost to someone.

The Jews at Capernaum apparently were looking for a free lunch, like the one their forefathers received. All the time the ancient Israelites had wandered in the desert, God had supplied their physical needs: He had sent them manna from heaven.

God's provision was memorialized for the Jews in the display of a carved manna pot by the lintel of the synagogue door. Upon seeing this stone pot, a worshiper would recall the miracle of God's daily supply. Excavations at Capernaum's synagogue have unearthed just such a manna pot. Perhaps it was this very pot that inspired Jesus' teaching about the true bread of heaven.

Compare the two. The manna that God freely gave to His wandering children in the desert was a physical bread from heaven. It lasted only one day. No matter how nutritious and delicious, it satisfied physical hunger for a brief period of time only.

Jesus declares that He is the spiritual bread come down from heaven. He supplies a gift that lasts forever. Those who by faith accept His bodily sacrifice for their sins are nourished spiritually. They will never be separated from God. This bread of heaven is also free, but it cost Jesus His life.

Jesus, as the living bread that comes down from heaven, offers us the free gift of everlasting spiritual life. The Jews did not understand the spiritual truth conveyed in these earthly terms. Do you?

Lord Jesus, you are the bread of heaven that gives me spiritual life. My soul is nourished as I feast on all that you are to me.

INSIGHT

Many fascinating archeological discoveries have been made at Tel Hum, identified by most as the site of New Testament Capernaum.

The impressive remains of a fourth-century synagogue cover the site where once an older synagogue stood. This is probably the spot where Jesus identified Himself as the bread of heaven. Perhaps it is the location of the synagogue that was built for the Jews by the Roman centurion mentioned in Luke 7:1–5. These ruins, though broken and battered, still display their ancient beauty.

Nearby, tradition says, is the house of St. Peter. This complex arrangement of black basalt stones bears witness to the centuries of building, remodeling, and destruction that have wreaked havoc on this site.

This milestone stands in Capernaum, an archeological remnant of the ancient roadway that once ran along the Mediterranean coast.

An olive mill and oil press were discovered here. A road marker from the old Roman highway tells of the strategic location Capernaum once enjoyed. Dozens of intricate carvings from the synagogue reveal the splendor of its ancient glory.

Beyond the wall to the north of the synagogue are additional Roman and Byzantine structures that many tourists miss. These ruins of a home, a bathhouse, a storehouse, and two public buildings are further evidence of Capernaum's former prominence.

ENRICHMENT

When you go to church today, the preacher stands, and the people sit. In Jesus' day, the rabbi sat down as he taught, and all the listeners stood. Try out the ancient way as you visit this centuries-old synagogue. If you have time, read more than just the ten suggested verses. John 6:25–59 reveals the whole context of Jesus' teaching on the bread of heaven.

Relationship of Love

When they had finished eating, Jesus said to Simon Peter, "Simon son of John, do you truly love me more than these?" "Yes, Lord," he said, "you know that I love you." Jesus said, "Feed my lambs."

John 21:15

Embedded in the Galilean shoreline by the Church of Peter's Primacy, these heart-shaped stones symbolize Jesus' timeless question: "Do you love me?"

It is hard to think of a more contemptible sin than Peter's threefold denial of Christ. Without a doubt, Peter was still embarrassed and ashamed when Jesus met him by the sea soon after the resurrection. Probably he was wondering what Jesus would say in that first personal conversation since his public denial.

Yet Jesus' words were gentle. They were to the point. And they did not dredge up Peter's sin. Instead they reestablished his relationship. They put the focus on love.

Perhaps it was because Peter denied Jesus three times that Jesus asked him three times, "Do you love me?" Maybe the repetition was necessary so that impetuous Peter was forced to think about his reply and be sure he meant it. Possibly Peter was made to repeat his answer because his threefold testimony was more binding. Whatever the reason, Jesus showed He was more concerned with restoring His relationship with Peter than with rehearsing his failures.

Amazingly, Jesus not only reinstated Peter to a position of leadership, but He also commissioned him to additional responsibilities. Peter now had the duty of feeding Jesus' sheep, a high privilege and serious obligation.

Sometimes we are slow to release our burdens of guilt. We allow our shame to stop our spiritual service. Certainly we must repent of our sin before we can be useful in ministry. But once we are forgiven, we need to get on with God's business. There is a kingdom job for every repentant sinner who still loves Jesus.

Gracious God, since you restored Peter to a loving relationship and gave him leadership responsibility, then there is hope also for me. As a forgiven follower I tell you again, "I love you." Please show me the ministry in which I now can serve you and prove my gratitude.

INSIGHT

The Church of Peter's Primacy is a simple black basalt box hugging the edge of the Sea of Galilee. Its foundations rest on the waterside rocks and its altar floor is known as Mensa Domini, "the Table of the Lord." Here the resurrected Christ is said to have eaten a breakfast of bread and broiled fish with His disciples. And here, according to Catholic teaching, Christ made Peter the head of the church.

ENRICHMENT

Like pendants from a broken necklace, a string of large heart-shaped stones lies half-embedded in the pebbles of the shore. Placed here long ago by some unknown devotee, they are tangible reminders of our need to answer Jesus' compelling question: "Do you truly love me?"

Gods of Convenience

After seeking advice, the king made two golden calves. He said to the people, "It is too much for you to go up to Jerusalem. Here are your gods, O Israel, who brought you up out of Egypt."

1 Kings 12:28

Among the significant discoveries at Tel Dan are the ruins of a horned altar. A replica of the altar can now be seen at the worship site.

Convenience is one of the new standards for the successful church. Build a facility that is visible and accessible. Provide surplus parking. Offer lots of options. Schedule worship services at convenient times.

All this is good. In an effort to meet the expectations of a convenience-oriented culture, the church must be willing to change forms without altering substance. As much as possible, it must adapt to the patterns of the people it is called to serve.

Convenience, however, can become a god itself. It is a sin to change the clear commandments of God in order to accommodate convenience. This was the sin of Jeroboam I, the first king of the northern kingdom of Israel.

To keep the people from traveling to Jerusalem to worship at the Temple, he set up golden calves in Bethel and Dan. He sold this worship innovation by billing it as more convenient, but his real purpose was political. He was afraid if the people went to Jerusalem, their allegiance to the house of David might be strengthened.

In the name of convenience, the king disregarded the clear commandment of Exodus 20:4: "You shall not make for yourself an idol." He overlooked the promise of blessing God put on the temple in Jerusalem. Consequently history remembers Jeroboam I as the prime example of an idolatrous king.

The leaders of the church today must be on guard against the gods of convenience. God never promised that worship of Him would be quick, easy, and convenient. In fact, Jesus said God is seeking those who will worship Him in spirit and in truth (John 4:24). Truth may cost. Sacrifice may be required. Commitment is often inconvenient, but we worship God—not convenience.

Lord, give me a heart that is fully devoted to you. Then I will worship in spirit and in truth without concern for convenience.

INSIGHT

Bible writers used the expression "from Dan to Beersheba" to indicate the whole of the country—from its northernmost city to its key southern settlement (Judges 20:1). Situated in the foothills of Mount Hermon, the ancient city of Dan once sat astride the principal source of the Jordan River.

Today a beautiful one-hundred-acre nature reserve (thought by some to be the location of the Garden of Eden) surrounds Tel Dan, the site of archeological excavations since 1965. The city gate, 65 x 85 feet (19 x 26 m), is the largest discovered to date in Israel.

ENRICHMENT

Ironically, though Jeroboam I made Dan a convenient worship center in the tenth century B.C. its location is too inconvenient for most tour groups today. However, the adventurous visitor is well-rewarded by the incomparable beauty and archeological significance of the site. Spend some quiet, worshipful moments under the leafy canopy of mulberry and fig trees. Imagine Adam and Eve walking with God in such a paradise as this.

Valley of Victory

Then they gathered the kings together to the place that in Hebrew is called Armageddon.

Revelation 16:16

The Jezreel Valley (viewed from Jezreel tel) lies in a strategic position between Galilee and Samaria.

The emerald mantle of the Jezreel Valley drapes itself across Israel's northern countryside. From the Mediterranean heights of Mount Carmel to the rushing waters of the Jordan, the nation's largest valley sprouts vegetables and fruit enough to feed thousands. But its soft green cloak covers a crimson past.

As the only natural east-west passageway across the nation, its broad back provided a ready battlefield for the clash of angry armies. The iron chariots of the Canaanites rolled easily over the level plain. And here, Gideon's brave band routed Israel's ancient enemies.

Evidence of the Jezreel Valley's gory history now erupts only briefly at such places as the chariot city of

Tel Megiddo. But one day, perhaps not too far in the future, this peaceful blanket of green will be torn again by the boots of soldiers and dipped in the blood of legions gathered to war against the King of kings.

Armageddon. That single word explodes with all manner of meaning, hard-packed by Bible interpreters over the centuries. Although it appears only once in all of Scripture, volumes have been written attempting to explain its significance. This much is sure: Armageddon stands for the final, decisive battle between the forces of this world, drawn together by Satan, against the Lord Jesus Christ. At the end of the Great Tribulation, the kings of the earth will gather to invade Israel and war against God. Then Christ will return to judge the nations, and the Jezreel Valley will become the valley of victory for Jesus our King.

My allegiance belongs to Jesus the King of kings. May I live today so that everyone will know which side I am on.

INSIGHT

The valley, which is now a source of life for all who feast upon its agricultural bounty, was once a place of death. Until reclaimed by Jewish settlers, the Jezreel Valley was a malarial swamp where millions of mosquitoes flourished. Now fifty years later, the area hums with humanity in the villages, kibbutzim, and tourist traffic.

ENRICHMENT

The Jezreel Valley may be viewed from many locations. Whether you gaze upon its expanse from Megiddo, Nazareth, or Beth Shan, pause long enough to envision the vast armies that one day will march across its now peaceful plain. Hear the clanging and clashing of forces in conflict. Smell the blood and sweat of death and destruction arising from the battlefield. See this verdant valley flush with a scarlet hue as God releases the vintage of His wrath on His enemies.

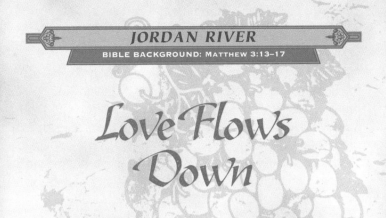

Love Flows Down

And a voice from heaven said, "This is my Son, whom I love; with him I am well pleased."

Matthew 3:17

The Jordan River snakes for more than 200 miles (320 km) between the Sea of Galilee and the Dead Sea.

Our Lord's journey to Calvary began on the banks of the Jordan. His baptism signified the beginning of His public ministry. The path of obedience led Jesus into the muddy waters of the River Jordan and up the steep slope of salvation.

Jordan means "going down." This most prominent river in the Bible descends from the snowy slopes of Mount Hermon in northern Israel to the Dead Sea. It drops 1570 feet (479 m) in a snake-like route extending nearly 240 miles (380 km). When it finally spills into the Dead Sea at 1285 feet (392 m) below sea level, the Jordan is the world's lowest river.

It is to this river, sometimes called "The Descender," that Jesus came to be baptized by John. The precise location of this momentous event was not recorded by any of the gospel writers. But Matthew, Mark, and Luke each faithfully recorded what they considered a much more significant fact: All three persons of the Trinity participated in this inauguration of Jesus' redemptive ministry.

Jesus' baptism was His public commitment to the divine plan of salvation. He understood the supreme sacrifice that He had to make. The Holy Spirit rested His comforting presence on Jesus and strengthened Him for what lay ahead. God the Father voiced His approval saying, "This is my Son, whom I love; with him I am well pleased."

The presence of the Father and the Holy Spirit at Jesus' baptism symbolizes the Trinity's full participation in our salvation. We are saved by Jesus' death, regenerated by the Spirit, according to the plan of the Father. Our salvation is a gift of God in unified fullness.

The love of God still flows through Jesus today. He longs to fill the heart of each one who will accept His gift of salvation.

To the Father, Son, and Holy Spirit, I lift my grateful heart. Your love flows down from heaven to bring salvation to the lowest sinner.

INSIGHT

Scholars debate whether Jesus' baptism took place in northern or southern Israel. Matthew's account says Jesus came from Galilee to the Jordan. Even more specifically, Mark says Jesus came from Nazareth in Galilee to the Jordan. This would seem to indicate He headed south, but just how far? The context of Luke's baptism account is interpreted by some to indicate a location nearer to the Dead Sea. Indeed, in the Jericho vicinity there are no fewer than seven shrines claiming to mark the place where Jesus was baptized. Apparently God's inspired plan is to leave the location vague. This way we are not tempted to revere the baptism location above the Lord Himself.

ENRICHMENT

Hundreds of people each year are baptized in the Jordan. There is a place specially prepared for baptisms near where the river flows out from the Sea of Galilee. If you want to be baptized here, you should make plans with your tour host before you leave home.

Capture your Jordan River experience and carry it home in a bottle. No doubt you will be drinking a lot of bottled water while in Israel, so save one of your empty bottles. Dip it into the Jordan and take back a liquid memento. Just be sure you label the bottle. If you drink it, you may get a whole lot more than you bargained for.

MEGIDDO

BIBLE BACKGROUND: JUDGES 5:1–5, 19–22, 31

Power for Victory

The horse is made ready for the day of battle, but victory rests with the Lord.

Proverbs 21:31

Remains of the ancient gateway discovered at Megiddo frame a view of the Esdraelon Plain, the central lowland of the Jezreel Valley.

Throughout Old Testament times, a poor man never owned a horse. They were the prize of the rich and powerful. Strong and fearless in battle, the horse was the symbol of power.

Perhaps for this reason, God gave His people special instructions about the horse. He specifically said the king was not to acquire great numbers of horses (Deuteronomy 17:16). God wanted the ruler of His chosen people to trust in Him rather than to rely upon the usual means of military strength.

King Solomon, however, paid no attention to God's prohibition. Instead, he amassed a force of twelve thousand horses and four thousand chariots. These he kept readied for battle in Jerusalem and the chariot cities of the north, including Megiddo.

No doubt Solomon thought the borders of his nation were securely protected by such mighty horsepower. But history proves otherwise. Shortly after his death, Megiddo fell into the hands of Israel's enemies. The thousands of horses and chariots assembled through disobedience were not enough to protect the city.

Today God's people are still tempted to trust tangible resources instead of God Himself. For example, retirement worries might drive some Christians to concentrate on amassing assets rather than to manage their God-given resources as the Lord directs: they hoard instead of give. It is possible to end up with large portfolios and push God out of the picture. Saving is not a sin. But we must be careful to make God our security rather than make securities our god.

The church's tendency is to rely on programs rather than spiritual power. While it may be wise to hire a consultant to help us raise money for a building project, the power does not reside in the prescribed plan. It takes more than merely following the manual. Spiritual power flows into the church through prayerful dependence on God.

Security is not found in numbers, be it horses or dollars. Success is not guaranteed by plans, programs, or people-power. Rather, as Solomon himself noted, "Victory rests with the Lord" (Proverbs 21:31).

God, help me to believe what your word tells me—victory comes from you. No strategy is effective without prayerful dependence on you.

INSIGHT

Megiddo has been called the crown jewel of biblical archeology in Israel. This thirteen-acre tel contains the secrets of more than twenty civilizations built on this site since about 4000 B.C. Extensive excavations have uncovered many major structures and revealed the life of its various inhabitants.

The ancient ruins of Megiddo include two clusters of buildings that are popularly identified as Solomon's Stables. Archeologists debate the date and use of these

This stone manger at Megiddo provides insight into what Christ's first cradle may have been like.

structures. However, many scholars estimate that if they were used as stables, they could have housed as many as 450 horses. Solid blocks of stone (3 x 2 x 1.5 feet; or 1 x .6 x .5 m) with scooped out, basin-like surfaces often are identified as mangers. Upright pillars have holes through them which might have been the tethering places for Solomon's horses.

Besides Solomon's Stables, you can see the ruins of an oval-shaped Canaanite altar nearly 26 feet (8 m) across and 5 feet (1.6 m) high. An underground water system reveals amazing ancient engineering. A grain silo dated to the eighth or ninth century B.C. could hold an estimated 12,800 bushels (450,000 l) of grain. All these, plus the ruins of a multi-chambered gate, a palace, pillars, and walls make Megiddo a treasure not to be missed.

ENRICHMENT

The wooden mangers you see in Christian art depicting Jesus' birth are fabrications of the artist's imagination. Because of the scarcity of trees in this rocky country, it is highly unlikely that animal feeding troughs would have been constructed from wood. It is much more likely that Jesus' manger was a stone one similar to those at Megiddo. In fact, other masonry mangers have been discovered elsewhere in Israel. In the Grotto of the Nativity in Bethlehem you can spot the area designated as the manger. It is stone.

Run your hand over the rough-hewn surface of the manger at Megiddo. Imagine placing your newborn there. Keep this picture in your mind. It is probably closer to reality than those you will find on your Christmas cards.

Life is Simple

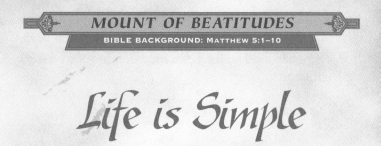

Now when he [Jesus] saw the crowds, he went up on a mountainside and sat down. His disciples came to him, and he began to teach them.

Matthew 5:1-2

This grassy hillside may be the one where Jesus taught the Sermon on the Mount, and at its summit a lovely octagonal church memorializes the eight beatitudes.

Great communicators make the complex simple. In the Beatitudes, Jesus, the greatest communicator, simplifies the complexity of life. He distills his divine expectations for the character and conduct of His disciples into eight simple statements. A brief overview reminds us that His expectations still apply.

The first step in following Jesus requires us to recognize our spiritual bankruptcy. Without Christ we have nothing to offer God. Our own goodness, merit, and morality fall short of His perfection. It is a blessed freedom to admit our inadequacy before God.

Seeing our spiritual poverty causes us to weep. A genuine mourning over our sinful condition results in a certain sorrow. This sorrow, however, leads us to repentance and thus to spiritual joy.

The third beatitude deals with the much misunderstood concept of meekness. The meek inherit the earth, but not because they are passive and weak. Meekness, rather, is strength under control, and God blesses that characteristic with great reward.

Do you hunger and thirst for righteousness? Jesus promises that when we are serious about doing what is right, He happily fills our spiritual desire.

In the fifth beatitude Jesus proclaims that we harvest what we sow. If we show mercy to others, we will receive mercy in return.

"Blessed are the pure in heart" carries its own reward. God does not look on the outward appearance but sees our inner spiritual condition. Likewise, when our inner attitude is pure, we are enabled to recognize more of who God is.

The seventh beatitude has special significance for the visitor to this strife-filled country. Today Israel is being pushed and pulled from all sides. Her enemies insist on more concessions and threaten war. Even those who love Israel disagree over which path leads to permanent peace. The peacemaker is a son of God because God himself has made peace with us through His Son Jesus Christ.

The final beatitude is so vital Jesus repeats it. In his kingdom, his subjects must display the same characteristics they see in their master. When we endure wrongful persecution, we find ourselves in good company with the prophets of old. And more meaningful is the fact that we prove we are ready for the kingdom of heaven.

On this mount He taught His first disciples eight simple rules for living a life that pleases God and honors

Jesus our Savior. In this same place Jesus can instruct you, too, if your heart is soft toward Him.

Jesus, when I listen quietly, my heart can hear you speak. The echoes of your words spoken in this place reach me now. Teach me the simple blessedness of living by your standard in my complex world today.

INSIGHT

Current tradition accepts the site near the Church of the Beatitudes as the location where Jesus delivered His Sermon on the Mount. It is a couple miles (3 km) southwest of and 368 feet (112 m) higher than Capernaum. This natural amphitheatre by the Sea of Galilee would have been easily accessible to Jesus and the throngs of followers.

The other suggested location is the Horns of Hattim, a twin-peak natural escarpment 8 miles (13 km) southwest of Capernaum. You will have to decide for yourself which of these two locations best fits the biblical context. A comparison of Mark 3:7-13, Luke 6:12-19, and Matthew 5:1 may provide some insights.

ENRICHMENT

There seems to be a church on every holy site in Israel. As beautiful as they are, they cannot compare to the natural beauty of what God has made. So once you have taken in the hillside view from the cloisters of the Church of the Beatitudes, ask your guide if you may go down into the meadow below.

Find a rock to sit on and tune in to the acoustics of this unique place. Can you hear the waves lapping at the foot of the hill? What other sounds can you detect from a distance? Listen to the birds. Then imagine this slope populated by the thousands who came to receive Jesus' ministry. Reading the Beatitudes in this natural setting will refresh your spirit like nothing else can.

Faith on Fire

[Elijah declared], "The god who answers by fire—he is God."
1 Kings 18:24

In this statue, Elijah brandishes his knife and fixes his foot on the neck of a defeated prophet of Baal.

Elijah, a common man with uncommon faith, yielded every advantage to his opponent, but still won the day. Let us examine the seven advantages the prophets of Baal had in their contest with Elijah, the prophet of God.

The most obvious advantage was *numbers*. It was 450 against 1. And it is clear from 1 Kings 18:22 that Elijah felt the loneliness of his isolation.

Yet it did not keep him from deliberately granting the prophets of Baal additional advantages. He gave his pagan opponents the opportunity of *choice* as to which sacrificial bull they wanted to use. Almost as if he wanted to eliminate any possibility of a charge of foul play, Elijah says, "Let them choose" (18:23).

Once the prophets of Baal started their rituals, they seemed to excel in other ways. Contrast their methods to those of Elijah. They had the advantage of *volume* (18:26-28). They shouted and prophesied with passion, but Elijah prayed with quiet confidence.

If wild activity was the gauge for *zeal*, then they appeared to possess more. They danced and frantically flagellated themselves to get the attention of their god. Elijah, on the other hand, did none of this. When it came his turn, he stepped forward with dignity and simply prayed (18:36).

The pagan prophets also escalated the confrontation beyond animal sacrifice when they spilled their own blood in their appeal to Baal (18:28). If *human blood* could gain favor, they had it. Elijah remained cool. He knew human sacrifice was abhorrent to his God.

Sixth, the prophets of Baal had the advantage of *time*. They churned and agitated themselves from morning until evening, trying everything they knew to get their god to respond (18:26-29). It went on for hours until Elijah finally stepped in and called a halt.

As if these six factors were not enough to guarantee the outcome, Elijah heightened the drama by directly handicapping himself. While the prophets of Baal had dry wood under their sacrifice, Elijah dowsed his offering with twelve large jars of water—so much water that it ran down around the altar and filled a trench (18:32–35).

Seven apparent advantages Elijah allowed his rival priests. But none of these could overcome the fact that Baal was impotent. Elijah worshiped the one true God, and his faith was white-hot. Nothing could quench its fervency.

God answered Elijah's faith with fire. Fire so consuming that it burned not only the wood and the sacrifice, but the stones, the soil, and the water as well! The people of Israel immediately fell on their faces to acknowledge that "The LORD—he is God! The LORD—he is God!"

This Mount Carmel contest appeared to be a setup for Elijah's downfall, but it turned out to be the venue for victory. Elijah's fervent faith was answered by fire, and God was glorified. When we are called upon to display intense faith, we must remember we serve a God who rewards faith with fire.

O Lord, my faith is too often feeble and faint. Create in me a fervent faith that you can answer with fire.

INSIGHT

Carmel means "God's vineyard" or "God's garden." Native flowers, vineyards, and fragrant evergreen forests make it a lush and lovely area. Being east of the Mediterranean, its 1500-foot (450 m) hills snag the rain clouds and draw down their moisture on the verdant slopes.

It is easy to see why Carmel was sacred to those who worshiped Baal, the Canaanite god of rain, weather, and storms. With 450 prophets of Baal and 400 prophets of Asherah (Baal's mother) close by, clearly this area was a pagan stronghold. Their defeat by Elijah proved our God is the One who "makes the clouds his chariot and rides on the wings of the wind. He makes winds his messengers, flames of fire his servants" (Ps. 104:3–4).

ENRICHMENT

A Roman Catholic monastery is located on Mount Carmel at the traditional site of the contest between Elijah and the prophets of Baal. In its courtyard stands a statue of the fiery prophet flashing a knife and taking the victor's pose over a defeated prophet of Baal. While there isn't a lot to see on the ground, there is a spectacular view from the monastery roof. To the east you can see the Jezreel Valley, the hills of Nazareth, and even Mount Gilboa.

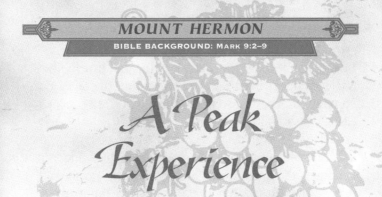

A Peak Experience

There he was transfigured before them. His clothes became dazzling white, whiter than anyone in the world could bleach them.

Mark 9:2–3

In the distance, Mount Hermon's hoary head collects the winter snows and sends them south to form the Jordan River.

The English poet William Blake observed, "Great things are done when men and mountains meet; / This is not done by jostling in the street." Indeed, the Bible repeatedly illustrates this truth. The Lord led Abraham to Mount Moriah, there to provide the sacrifice that spared Isaac's life. On the slopes of Mount Horeb, God appeared to Moses in the burning bush, and then atop Mount Sinai, He delivered the Ten Commandments into Moses' hands.

Mount Carmel saw the victory of the one true God over Baal's deluded prophets. And the Mount of Olives hosted many marvelous events in the life of Christ, including His ascension into heaven.

Likewise both Matthew and Mark point out that Jesus' transfiguration took place on a high mountain. Whether the referenced peak is Mount Hermon (the highest and closest mountain) or Mount Tabor (the traditional place) cannot be settled with certainty. Whichever site is right, its lofty and lonely location provided the proper venue for a private display of Christ's glorious divinity shining through His sinless humanity. The transfiguration surely was one of the greatest things ever done when men and mountains meet.

Here the three disciples were treated to a glimpse of God's glory and a foretaste of heaven. They witnessed a metamorphosis in which the inner divinity of Christ's nature transformed His outward appearance. His personal purity radiated from His physical form with such brilliance that Mark seems to strain for words. This, along with the appearance of Moses and Elijah and the affirmation from the Father, convinced the disciples of Christ's full divinity.

Revelations such as this may come to modern-day followers of Jesus, too. Some occur during mountain retreats. Others result from a walk with the Shepherd in the valley of shadows. Wherever these spiritual discoveries take place, they mark a high point in the believer's spiritual walk and a pinnacle along the path of discipleship.

Lord Jesus Christ, may the radiance of your glory blind me to all rival gods. I want my life to be marked by having met with you on the mountain top.

INSIGHT

The gospel writers agree that the transfiguration of Christ took place shortly after Peter's affirmation of Jesus as the "Christ, the Son of the Living God." Although the

Mount of Transfiguration is not named in any biblical text, Mount Hermon is a logical choice. Its triple summit rises less than a day's journey north from Caesarea Philippi where Peter made his declaration. This limestone massif is Israel's highest mountain, rising over 9200 feet (2800 m) above sea level. Snowcapped most of the year, it may be the only Holy Land peak that can rightfully be called a high mountain.

ENRICHMENT

Wherever you are in Galilee, keep an eye out for Mount Hermon's hoary head. You can spot it from many locations. On a clear day it can be seen from as far south as the Dead Sea.

Today a modern ski resort clings to one side of the mountain's face. Although it is not much by way of comparison to the famous ski slopes of Europe or the United States, it affords a refreshing getaway in winter and a cool retreat in summer.

The Christian traveler can see in the white snows of Hermon a reminder of the purity of the Savior's life and a symbol of the cleansing offered to every repentant sinner. Through Christ, our sins, though red like scarlet, shall be as white as snow (Isaiah 1:18).

Low Expectations

He did not do many miracles there because of their lack of faith.
Matthew 13:58

Beneath the limestone cliffs, the Church of the Annunciation (center) dominates the town of Nazareth.

Long before Jesus' time, Aesop was teaching that familiarity breeds contempt. Perhaps that is the reason Jesus received no respect from the people of His hometown. They felt they knew too much about Jesus to expect great things from Him.

Researchers estimate that no more than fifty families lived in Nazareth during Jesus' boyhood years. This small town in the hills of Galilee was the perfect atmosphere for mediocrity to flourish. Everyone knew everyone. Everyone knew everyone's business. Everyone knew everyone's abilities. Therefore, everyone expected everyone to be just like everyone else.

When Jesus moved away from Nazareth to begin His public ministry, He had not been voted "Most Likely to Succeed." Indeed, as the locals saw it, He had three strikes against Him.

First, His family was common. Joseph was just a carpenter—a man with a manual trade. While we might like to think that he was a dedicated worker with exceptional skill and integrity, we have no evidence to prove it. On the contrary, the people of Nazareth considered Joseph "just one of us." His mother's name, Mary, was shared by many other women. And, since Jesus' half brothers and half sisters still lived in the area, they also provided the standard by which Jesus Himself was judged.

Second, His schooling was average. When Jesus taught with authority in their synagogue, His hearers were amazed. They asked, "Where did this man get this wisdom?" (see Matthew 7:28–29). They knew that their teachers and synagogue rulers didn't dispense this kind of knowledge and understanding.

Third, His powers were normal, as far as they were concerned. It is an ironic testimony to the humanity of Jesus Christ that His hometown observers saw Him as average. Evidently He had never used His divine powers to perform cute tricks and impress His boyhood companions. And now when He returned to Nazareth on a wave of notoriety and with tales of miracles in His wake, they simply refused to believe it. They did not want to accept Jesus for anything more than what He seemed to be while He was growing up. In fact, they were offended that He now exceeded their low expectations.

Matthew delivers the God-inspired commentary on this case when he records that Jesus did not do many miracles in Nazareth because the people lacked faith. They could not or would not see Jesus for all He really was—the Messiah sent to save them. Thus they missed an encounter with the one who was able to do immeasurably more than all they could ask or imagine.

Jesus, I confess that like the people of Nazareth I, too, am guilty of low expectations. Help me grow in my faith. Then, when I raise my eyes to heaven, I will also raise my expectations.

INSIGHT

Jesus lived most of His life in Nazareth. Except for a few days in Bethlehem and a brief sojourn in Egypt, Nazareth was Jesus' home until He was thirty. At that time He left His boyhood home and moved to Capernaum.

Thirty years in a very small town. Many memories were made here as the boy Jesus "grew in wisdom and stature, and in favor with God and men" (Luke 2:52). Although the Bible records very little of Jesus' growing-up years, the Christians of Nazareth claim to have discovered a lot.

Every view of Nazareth is dominated by the magnificent Church of the Annunciation, the largest Christian church building in the Middle East. Completed in 1969, it is the fifth church built on the traditional spot where the angel Gabriel prophesied to Mary that she would bear the Messiah. Here also is a place known as Joseph's Workshop (also called Carpenter Shop of Joseph), over which the Church of St. Joseph is built, supposedly on the site of the holy family's home.

The synagogue where Jesus learned the law and later interpreted the prophets is in Nazareth. But no one can be certain which of several suggested locations is correct. Luke writes that the townspeople were so furious when Jesus applied Isaiah's prophecy to Himself, that they tried to throw Him off a cliff. Alas, even this site is in dispute.

The thing to remember about Nazareth is that, even though specific sites are debatable, the general location is indisputable. This *is* Jesus' hometown.

ENRICHMENT

Try to imagine what it must have been like for Jesus to grow up in the small village of Nazareth. While you tour the town, look around you. Keep your eyes open to the faces of the people who live there today. Do you expect anyone great to come out of Nazareth?

High-Visibility Christianity

You are the light of the world. A city on a hill cannot be hidden.
Matthew 5:14

The quaint houses and narrow streets of Safed lend to the mystique of this city on the hill.

Though salt may work its savor while hidden and unseen, light is most effective when visible and bright. Maximum visibility means maximum value. The light *of* the world must be visible *to* the world.

While elsewhere Jesus affirms the value of anonymous good deeds done in secret, here He emphasizes the opposite. An oil lamp placed on a high stand lights a room well. A city on a summit is seen from miles around. Good deeds done publicly bring praise to God from a larger audience.

Admittedly some Christians struggle with this concept. They perceive public good deeds as motivated by pride. They condemn the conspicuous as sinful. But Jesus' command to "let your light shine" is a clear mandate for high-visibility Christianity.

High-impact Christianity is a collective accomplishment. It is not achieved alone.

Every time the pronoun *you* or *your* appears in these four verses, it is plural. Our English translations fail to convey this crucial point. Jesus does not say individual Christians are to be lights in the world. Alone, a single candle cannot dispel the world's darkness. Rather Jesus stresses the collective value of many lights shining together. The greater the number, the greater the impact will be.

A city on a hill is not noted at night because of a single little lamp, no matter how prominently displayed. A city is luminous because of the collective intensity of many lights shining together.

Christians working together produce a greater impact on society than any one alone. And when they work together publicly, they have the greatest effect.

Lord, I understand that one light does not make a city bright; but I pledge to work together with other believers, so that together we may make a difference in our world for you.

INSIGHT

At 2736 feet above sea level, Safed is Israel's highest city. During the day its white stone buildings gleam in the sunlight. At night it sparkles with light. Probably it was to this city that Jesus referred when He taught His disciples the value of their collective light in the world.

Safed is only one version of the name for this quaint village northwest of the Sea of Galilee. It is variously spelled *Safad, Sefat, Tsfat, Tzfat, Zefat* and *Zfat*. Since different maps and references use different English transliterations, you may have to look twice before you find it.

Under any name, Safed is one of Judaism's four holy cities. (Tiberias, Hebron, and Jerusalem are the others.) It has a centuries-old reputation as a center for Jewish mysticism. Several great rabbis are buried in the cemetery on nearby Mount Meron.

ENRICHMENT

Today one of Safed's chief attractions is its artists' colony. With over fifty artists living in this picturesque mountain town, paintings, sculpture, and prints abound. If you travel to Safed take time to sample its many galleries, cafes, and shops.

Stormy Weather

He replied, "You of little faith, why are you so afraid?" Then he got up and rebuked the winds and the waves, and it was completely calm.

Matthew 8:26

The beauty of the Sea of Galilee is surpassed only by its bounty.

Mark Twain said, "Everybody talks about the weather, but nobody does anything about it!" That is because nobody *can* do anything about it. The weather is beyond human control. But as Jesus showed His disciples, even the weather was under His divine control.

The disciples obediently shoved off from the shore, not knowing what they were getting into. Part way across the lake a sudden storm swept down on them. Its suddenness and its severity were double cause for alarm.

Such quick changes in weather are common on the Sea of Galilee. Being 685 feet (209 m) below sea level and virtually surrounded by cliffs and hills, this small lake is subject to sudden weather changes. Cool air from the hills clashes with the warm moist air over the lake, and storms are created.

This squall swept the disciples (at least four of them veteran fishermen) right over their threshold of fear. They tolerated all they could, and when they saw no other way of escaping alive, they woke Jesus. "Lord, save us! We're going to drown!" they cried.

As Jesus awoke, the focus of His concern was not the wildness of the storm, but the weakness of the disciples' faith. He first rebuked them; then He rebuked the wind and the waves.

Calm and quiet were immediate. When nature stills a storm, the wind dies down first and eventually the waves stop rocking. But in this case, the miracle was so complete that Jesus stopped even the sloshing of the waves against the side of the boat. Matthew reported that there was complete calm.

This was a new category of miracle. An hour before, the disciples had not believed Jesus could control the weather. Now their faith in their Master was enlarged. He was able to do what no one else could. Even the wind and the waves obeyed His command.

The crisis served to strengthen their faith. Because they had been with Jesus in the storm, they were better equipped to follow Him as they stepped out onto dry land.

Lord Jesus, help me view each crisis in my life as an opportunity to increase my faith. As you quiet the wind and waves, calm my quaking heart. I need to know you are in command of even those things that no one else can control.

The Sea of Galilee is referred to by many names in the Bible. Because of its harp shape, the Old Testament calls it the Sea of Kinnereth (*kinnereth* is derived from the Hebrew word for harp [Numbers 34:11; Joshua 12:3]). Sea of Galilee is the most common name in the New Testament, though sometimes John calls it the Sea of Tiberias (21:1). One time, Luke refers to it as the Lake of Gennesaret (5:1).

Although relatively small (13 x 7.5 miles or 21 x 12 km), the Sea of Galilee is a significant part of the economy of Israel. It provides most of the fresh water for the nation. Its waters are used to irrigate the fertile western slopes, allowing them to produce abundant crops of grains, fruits, and vegetables. At least twenty-two

A local fisherman tends his nets on the Sea of Galilee with the Golan Heights as a backdrop.

species of fish swim in the Sea, providing the base for the area's thriving fishing industry.

Bible students note that ten of Jesus' thirty-three recorded miracles took place in the vicinity of this little lake. It was the backdrop for the first two years of our Lord's ministry. This is the place where Jesus fished, sailed, and stilled the tempest. He even walked on the Sea of Galilee.

ENRICHMENT

In 1986 a severe drought seized Galilee. The level of the Sea of Galilee slipped so low it revealed the hull of a boat that sailed these waters in Jesus' day. A replica of this first-century craft sails the Sea of Galilee today providing tourists a ride rich in memories and spiritual experience.

Your guide can arrange an excursion on this ship. If you go, ask the captain to cut the motors long enough for you to read the suggested Scripture and pray. As you drift quietly on this mirror of blue, cast your cares into the lap of the Lord who controls wind, waves, and weather. He is able to speak peace into your troubled heart.

More With Less

The Lord said to Gideon, "With the three hundred men that lapped I will save you and give the Midianites into your hands. Let all the other men go, each to his own place."

Judges 7:7

The cool waters of the Spring of Harod satisfied the thirst and tested the character of Gideon's men.

Common wisdom says "more is better." Given the option of having much food or little, we would all say "more is better." Given the choice for more money or less, we would quickly choose more. If preparing for war, we would recruit more manpower, not less.

Such was the case for Gideon. Faced with fighting the joint forces of "all the Midianites, Amalekites and other eastern peoples" (6:33), Gideon was glad to have thirty-two thousand troops show up ready for battle. Yet God told him there were too many soldiers.

So began a soldier-sifting process. "Send home all who tremble with fear," God said, and twenty-two thousand departed. "Now separate those who lap water from their cupped hands from those who kneel down to drink." This eliminated ninety-seven hundred more. In the end, Gideon's army was less than one percent of its initial force.

Why did God insist on paring the army's size so severely? Because in God's economy, more is not always better. Sometimes less is better. God often wants to show us He can do more with *less*.

In our churches, more is not always better. God can use a faithful, fearless few to storm the gates of hell. He can enable a small band of prayer warriors to prevail against innumerable hosts of evil. He is able to save, whether by many or by few.

God knew that if Israel was allowed to defeat the Midianites with many soldiers, they would attribute the victory to their own military might. In order to assure His divine glory, He had to ensure their human humility.

Sometimes God desires to decrease our strength so His divine glory may increase. Our almighty God is able to do more with less.

Lord, I confess my natural desire is always for more. Yet I acknowledge that you sometimes want to prove your power by doing more with less. Help me to accept your sifting as a sign that you want me to rely upon your strength.

INSIGHT

The Spring of Harod still bubbles from the mouth of a cave at the foot of Mount Gilboa in lower Galilee. Not only was it the scene of God's sifting of Gideon's army, but its waters have been the venue for other military ventures.

Many scholars speculate that this is the spring where Saul camped with his men before their fatal battle with the Philistines (1 Samuel 29:1). In addition, we know it was the site where in 1260 the Mameluks halted the invasion of the Mongols. Most recently, a secret Jewish self-defense team, including Moshe Dayan, trained near here just prior to Israel's independence in 1948.

ENRICHMENT

Ironically, the place where thousands of troops have gathered for war is now a peaceful picnic spot complete with a large swimming pool fed by the Spring of Harod. This small national park is carpeted with lush green lawns and guarded by towering eucalyptus trees. A gravel path leads to the open mouth of a small cave and a placid pool lying under its limestone lip.

A rivulet, cool and clear, flows from the cavern. Rest on the rocks beside this quiet stream. Plunge your hand into its refreshing waters. Remind yourself that you serve the same great God who saved His people from their enemies by the hand of Gideon and his small band.

Figure on Faith

Philip answered him, "Eight month's wages would not buy enough bread for each one to have a bite!"

John 6:7

The loaves and fishes mosaic memorializes Jesus' miraculous feeding of the five thousand which tradition says took place beside this rock, now incorporated in the altar of the Church of Heptapegon.

When faced with the challenge of feeding more than 5000 people, the disciples choked. They calculated the cost but failed to exercise faith.

This miracle is uniquely significant because it is the only one recorded in all four gospels. Although each writer adds different details, they all agree on the numbers: Five loaves and two fish are all they had to feed 5000 men.

Impossible! Philip and the disciples knew it. Jesus knew it, too. He asked Philip where to buy bread in order to evoke a spiritual response. Instead, Philip answered with figures rather than faith.

Do you respond the same way? Jesus asks you to give, and you calculate what it will cost you. He calls you to share, and you estimate the loss. He wants you to help, and you worry about how much.

Our tendency is to protect what we have, thinking that stewardship is synonymous with conservation. Stewardship, rather, means making our God-given resources available so the Lord can use them. Release brings increase in God's economy.

In tests of faith, the young sometimes perform better. Here a little boy was willing to surrender all he had into the hands of Jesus. The older and presumably wiser disciples wanted to discount his gift. Yet it was this small gift, given with 100 percent faith, that Jesus used to feed the multitudes

This miracle of multiplication is not about facts and figures. It is about faith. We must give Jesus all we are and all we have—no matter how inadequate it seems. He will make it more than enough.

Lord Jesus, I give you all I have. Use it for your purposes. Although my resources are meager, you are mighty.

INSIGHT

Tabgha is the Arabic form of the Greek word *heptapegon*, meaning seven springs. Located on the north shore of the Sea of Galilee, it is the site of both fresh and mineral springs. Since a principal ancient trade route skirted these shores, thousands of travelers tested these bubbling waters each year seeking relief from various ailments. Some believe this explains why over 5000 people were so near at hand to what the Bible calls a remote place.

Those hoping for temporary help discovered Jesus. He dispensed healing (Matthew 14:14), food, and wisdom (Mark 6:34). No wonder they thought he was wonderful. No wonder they wanted to make him king.

The next day, however, they found Jesus' primary concern was not for their physical needs. He wanted to heal them spiritually, feed them spiritually, and teach them spiritual truth. Ironically, in their search for a source of temporary relief, they stumbled upon the Source of eternal help. Sadly, most turned their backs on Jesus. They chose momentary comfort and rejected abundant life.

ENRICHMENT

The Church of the Loaves and Fishes (also known as the Church of Heptapegon) is built over the remains of two other churches. Some of the beautiful mosaic floors of the original building remain. Of course you will want to photograph the centuries-old mosaic of the loaves and fishes. Other designs feature flowers, flamingos, and cormorants.

This is a lovely place to spend a few moments in worship. The old hymn "Break Thou the Bread of Life" is a prayer that has special meaning in this location. The Lord who multiplied the little boy's lunch into enough for a multitude still works miracles today.

Recognizing Jesus

When they had rowed three or three and a half miles, they saw Jesus approaching the boat, walking on the water; and they were terrified. But he said to them, "It is I; don't be afraid."

John 6:19–20

The city of Tiberias, positioned on the southwestern shore of the Sea of Galilee, fascinates the visitor with an eclectic mix of new and old.

Seeing is not always believing. In fact, many times the disciples saw but disbelieved. On the Sea of Galilee after a hard night of desperate effort against a formidable storm, the twelve in the boat did not believe their own eyes when they saw Jesus coming to them walking on the water.

Who would blame them? They had never seen anyone walk on water, let alone Jesus, so it is understandable that they failed to recognize their Master. More than that, however, Matthew and Mark tell us the tired twelve thought they had seen a ghost.

Now a ghost generally does one of two things: it either haunts us or harms us.

A haunting ghost reminds us of our past. It rehearses our faults and recalls our failures. Unable to change the past, we may wallow in guilt and regret.

Furthermore, a ghost might bring harm in many ways. It might scare us about the future, terrify us with worry, or alarm us over events beyond our control. The result would be to destroy hope and discourage faith.

Jesus, however, emerged from the gray mist with a word of hope. He came to help. He reassured them saying, "It is I; don't be afraid."

Interestingly, though the disciples had seen Jesus, they had denied Him entrance into their boat to that point. They were so scared they refused to let Him get close. They failed to recognize the very one who was the answer to their prayers.

Finally, with recognition came help. At last Jesus brought peace to their souls, rest to their aching muscles, and calm to their circumstances.

How many times have we refused Jesus' help because we didn't recognize Him? Perhaps He didn't meet our expectations. Maybe He looked different than we thought He should. Possibly He appeared in an unusual place or arrived at an inconvenient time.

It might help us to recognize Jesus more readily if we begin to expect the unusual. It seems to be His trademark.

Jesus, I don't want to miss you just because you operate in a way I find unusual. Instead, help me to expect the exceptional and see you in the sensational.

INSIGHT

Although Tiberias was a busy seaport town in Jesus' day, the Bible mentions it only once in John 6:23. Apparently this is because Jesus avoided the city. Built by Herod Antipas as the capital for his administration of Galilee, it was essentially non-Jewish. Jesus focused His ministry on the Jews first (Matthew 15:24).

Things have changed since Jesus' day, however. Now Judaism considers this city of thirty-five thousand one of its four holy cities. The Mishnah was completed here in A.D. 200 and later the Jerusalem Talmud. Several revered rabbis are buried here.

ENRICHMENT

Tiberias offers a wide range of experiences. The traveler may choose a quiet stroll on the seaside promenade, a relaxing bath in the hot springs, or raucous night life. However, the Christian pilgrim may find *The Galilee Experience* to be both entertaining and instructive. This multimedia production employs twenty-seven projectors and thousands of images to tell the story of Tiberias and the Galilee in only thirty-six minutes.

SCRIPTURE INDEX

To locate verses that appear at the top of each day's devotional, see the Scripture below set in bold type. All other references correspond with verses used within the devotionals.

Jeff Baxter 11, 13, 22, 26, 29, 33, 39, 42, 44, 45, 54, 57, 61, 73, 75, 83, 85, 103, 115, 119, 122, 143, 151, 153, 155, 157, 167, 174, 177, 186, 196, 203, 205, 213

Timothy Beals 77, 169, 189

Evelyn Brown 36, 210

Charlene Davis 35, 106, 110, 179, 193

Linden Kirby 19, 30, 51, 64, 88, 94, 100, 125, 136, 138, 146, 161, 164, 171, 207

Israel Ministry of Tourism 140

Ila Prentiss 48

Phoenix Data Systems 16, 67, 91, 97, 113, 117, 128, 130, 132, 182, 184

Dorothy Russell 70

John Wendel 200

NOTES